Freemasons

A Study Of Constitutional Laws, Usages
And Landmarks Of Freemasons

(Unlock The Secrets Of Mysterious Society)

Juan Romine

Published By **Phil Dawson**

Juan Romine

Freemasons: A Study Of Constitutional Laws, Usages And Landmarks Of Freemasons (Unlock The Secrets Of Mysterious Society)

ISBN   978-1-77485-596-6

No part of this guidebook shall be reproduced in any form without permission in writing from the publisher except in the case of brief quotations embodied in critical articles or reviews.

Legal & Disclaimer

information provided by this guide. This disclaimer applies to any damages or injury caused by the use and application, whether directly or indirectly, of any advice or information presented, whether for breach of contract, tort, negligence, personal injury, criminal intent, or under any other cause of action.

You agree to accept all risks of using the information presented inside this book. You need to consult a professional medical practitioner in order to ensure you are both able and healthy enough to participate in this program.

Table of contents

Introduction

Freemasons Hall situated in London

For a long time, parodies involving the eerie and mysterious cults have long been the most popular gags within pop culture. The fraternal brothers are typically depicted as being in an underground cavern and dressed in elaborate ceremonial robes , with their faces concealed in jackets, seated around the table, which is filled with Gothic skulls, chalices and shimmering dark treasure. Some flicks on the more gruesome side may even be choppy flashing images of torture, blood and sacrifices.

As with all art forms, creativity is ignited by inspiration from a source and one of the most well-known people who inspire these scenes is the Freemasons. The ancient group, derived from the ancient tradition in stonemasonry believed to be the most profound darkest, most sinister, and mysterious truths about the universe. They are believed to possess magical powers unlike others or even magical powers. But does this stigmatization of the brotherhood actually have any merits or are they untruly misunderstood?

As most people are aware, Freemasons have existed for a long time. The Renaissance which was in full bloom in the 16th and 14th centuries witnessed a surge in the imagination and innovation in a variety of art forms across Europe. Stonemason guilds were able to ride the changing tides, and the new apprentices did not need to be confined by the trade. Many of the new apprentices were free-thinkers and artists yet they remained determined to stick to the tradition-based stone-cutter practices. The new generation of masons was distinct from traditional "operative" masonry and began to develop what came to be known as "speculative" masonry.

Like many legends, the roots of Freemasonry are not fully understood until today. The first reference to the fraternity dates its roots to The Halliwell Manuscript, or Regius Poem, which was believed to have been written sometime in the late 14th and early 15th century. The manuscript, written in beautiful Middle English and calligraphy, was comprised of 64 pages with 794 rhyme lines. It is regarded as to be the first of the renowned Masonic manuscripts, and it is widely accepted to be the "truthful" background of the fraternity's origins. The poem concerned begins with Euclid the Greek mathematician of around the fourth century BCE and is known today for being the "father of geometrical thinking." Math wizard was believed to have integrated geometric science into a new area he called "masonry." In this brand new and sophisticated version of scientific knowledge, Euclid went to Egypt and taught his knowledge to the kids from Egyptian nobles.

Chapter 1: The Beginning

One of the most elusive mysteries of the Freemasons is their history. Since the beginning of time there has been a debate in a tussle over when the order was created and who founded it. There are a myriad of competing theories, numerous unproven theories, and a few plain forgeries. The question of where the idea came from is a huge one. Although we may today have a current version of the Freemasons capable of functioning completely independent of the activities from a secret group that was established several centuries ago, some individuals believe it was those who founded the Order who laid the philosophical foundation, and thus the purpose and direction of the Freemasons. If we are to comprehend the Freemasons we need to comprehend the origins of their existence.

However, that's not to suggest that we need to pick a single view and adhere to it. The contrary the stories that tell the story of the origin of the Freemasons could be very helpful in our efforts to discover the reasons what the reasoning behind this particular order is so divided and controversial. The variations between the various versions of the origin story that people believe in will usually be a reflection of their personal beliefs and prejudices. For instance people who believe the Freemasons are the part of the Knights Templar may prefer be of the opinion that the Order continues to guard its old secrets. However, individuals who are of the opinion that this Order was a gentleman's group that was founded during the Eighteenth Century, seem far away from the more controversial beliefs about members of the Masonic Order. Therefore, by researching the many different historical sources, we will begin to understand and gain an understanding of why and how the opinions of Freemasons differ widely.

In the end, by studying the story of the Freemasons, we are able to get a distinct understanding of their role in our world of today. This means that although not every story of the historical organization of Freemasons is accurate but it is true that the tales have been a part of the public opinion about the order provides some knowledge. When we understand the stories that aren't real, and those that are, we can formulate our own opinions and gain an improved, more unified understanding. Like always, the truth always lies in the middle ; and the tale of the Freemasons can be an obscure, shady narrative with shades of gray. With no definitive heroes or villains Some people may find it difficult to grasp the truth of the matter. So, it is important to learn more about every aspect of Masonic history rather than only the highlights.

This is the reason it's best to begin at the beginning. However in the event that the time of the Order of the Freemasons is discussed, telling the whole and complete story may be difficult. In such instances it's helpful to consider a chronological approach. While the time period of Masons typically involves completely diverse individuals, some of whom would never ever heard of the term 'Freemasons Knowing about the background of this group will provide an understanding of the time when the major players begin to emerge. Freemasonry didn't come from the ashes of the world in a complete state. The creation of the Order (whenever it was) occurred as a result of a variety of forces and movements. The world events conspired to the formation of the Freemasons and, therefore, if we are to fully understand where the origins of the order are, we must attempt to understand the history in greater depth. That means we'll need to travel back in time hundreds of years to a different world from the modern world.

The history of Freemasonry is a legends. For a long time, for centuries, the Freemasons remained in existence. Although many knew they existed, there was no information about where they'd been from or what the catalyst for their creation. This changed towards the end in the Seventeenth Century, however. Masons in the Seventeenth Century began to question their origins and began to research the origins of their members. Through time this inquiry into the past was expanded to include non-Masons as well as those who were not involved in or were skeptical of Masonry. Thus the more comprehensive and more precise historical portrait of the group began to appear. But the details are being debated. To determine the most ancient and reliable source, we'll need to trace the history back to medieval times.

If you've spent more that 10 minutes studying on the Masons online, you'll encounter one name repeatedly and over: the Knights Templar. In reality, they are firmly woven into the tale of the Masons. But, their connection is sometimes disputed. The only thing we know is the fact that Knights Templar are credited with their involvement in the creation of Freemasons. The question is whether this is true or not, as the theory is widely believed and widely accepted, it is important to spend some time researching this group of Knights Templar, so that we will be able to be able to better understand what it is about this group that has people so keen to link their history to Masons and their past. The history about the Knights Templar is complicated and debated in its own way however the story is fascinating.

The Knights Templar

The Knights Templar have inspired hundreds perhaps thousands, of books written about the topic about the Knights Templar. They are awe-inspiring to people in a manner unlike any other organization and that is not even the Freemasons. Because the two groups have been among the more well-known and interesting of their genre and are awe-inspiring, it is to be only natural for them to be connected. Additionally, the merging of the stories of both organizations suggests that our tale will go far more distantly in the past. To uncover the authentic roots to the Knights Templar We must go back to the beginning of the millennium prior.

The story starts by describing the Crusades. An Holy War fought between the Catholic Church and the first version of Islam and the Islamic faith, there was a dispute regarding the character of the area in itself. To summarize (and to be a disservice to the rich culture in the capital city), Jerusalem became a important geopolitical problem. Since both major religions lay claim to the land as sacred (as as Judaism another faith in the same way) and there were regular conflicts over who was to have control over the city. For centuries the power ebbed and flowed through the region. When we begin the story around 1095 Jerusalem is under rule under the control of Muslim rulers.

As with many historical events, the circumstances were tense. It is beyond the subject matter of this book to discuss the many differences and disputes between the parties. For instance, the first principle to prevent the invasion of the Holy Lands by the westerners was to aid the Byzantine Emperor in his fight against an attack from Seljuk Turks. In time, as The Papacy and other major Western states joined in and the fight escalated into a larger campaign to take back Jerusalem and its surrounding areas that were under Muslim control from the 7th century onwards. In addition, the various conflicts of power among those Western royal houses resulted in certain rulers were eager to conduct campaigns of military force, while others wanted to be admired by Church leaders, while then there were some who were enticed to join due to other motivations or obligations.

The main point is that the Holy Lands, sometimes referred to as the Levant, became a focal point for a newly-formed Christian army. The Crusaders who were later known, travelled across Britain, France, Germany and Italy (as as from other states) through the land. On the way there were numerous incidents, among them a major and brutal attack on an Jewish group in Rhineland. The violence on the road could set the scene towards the final arrival to Jerusalem.

The First Crusade (there would be more to be added) was conducted as an actual military battle. When the Crusaders traveled from city to city from areas such as Antioch and Nicaea they laid an attack on and took over important cities, towns and castles. It took years to accomplish this, and numerous lives lost. However, finally they reached Jerusalem. Jerusalem.

In the midst of a siege on the Holy City in 1099, the Crusaders were confronted with challenging terrain. Outside City, landscape was arid desert. There was not much in the in the way of food or water and, far from their homes the people were in desperate need of food. With no time, depleted of supplies and power They were unable completely protect the city and stop the supply of food from entering. While they began their mission with tens thousands of troops including many riding on horses They were now down to 12,000 with only 1500 of them cavalrymen. The men remaining, drawn from various nations and backgrounds. They were in camp at the moment, and their morale was at a low.

The initial assault against the walls was rebuffed. They then attempted to walk around the walls while chanting at the top of their lungs following an intense three-day fast. The idea was for the building to fall as the biblical tale of Jericho. It didn't happen. After hearing of a second Muslim army leaving Egypt to fend off the Crusaders A final assault on Jerusalem was necessary. On July 15th the double-pronged attack against the city forced soldiers to flee the city. The crusaders remained inside.

It was followed by a bloody massacre. The Crusaders were marching for many years, traveling many miles, and losing many of their friends on the way in pursuit of capturing Jerusalem. The bloodbath is now a legend due to its brutality and barbarism. Perhaps the most significant--at least according to the narrative we're telling, were the events at Temple Mount. A lot of defenders were believed to have sought refuge at the site, which was among the top sacred spots around the globe. Temple Mount was vital to the three major Abrahamic religions. It is home to the al-Aqsa Mosque, the Dome of the Rock and the Dome of the Chain. The legend says that the biblical character Solomon created his own temple in this area that was destroyed and rebuilt a variety of times. For Muslims this is the third most sacred place in the world. It is the location from where Muhammad was able to ascend to heaven. In the days when the Crusaders were advancing, it was an appropriate place to seek refuge.

The Crusaders were on the lookout for and cut down any person they came across. Finally, a pause was commanded from the commander, which allowed those who had sheltered inside Al-Aqsa mosque to be sheltered. Al-Aqsa Mosque to be rescued. They would remain there for the duration of an entire day, the Crusader leaders waiting for the time when the streets in Jerusalem were swollen with blood prior to entering the mosque to kill the people who were sheltering. When the Crusaders were able to take over Jerusalem and started to establish the kingdom of Jerusalem The city was dealing with bloodshed on a massive size. Many were killed, and several were wounded. A world away from their home and the

Crusaders were busy with the task of governing in the Holy Land.

This was the place into that the Knights Templar were born. After the savage defeat of Jerusalem, Christianity now had control over one of the most sacred religious places. It was now crucial for those who wanted to demonstrate their faith in Jesus Christ. It was a time when the only option to travel for instance from France to Jerusalem was by the foot for those poor) or with horses for the rich or via boat for those who were wealthy and lucky. It is evident that this was a long journey and dangerous. Additionally, the violence that was that was left in the wake of the Crusade did not exactly bring Christians to the local communities they traveled by throughout the Levant region. Although Jerusalem could have been under the supervision of the Christians however, the area around was not so secure.

Infested by thieves, bandits and others who held an ill-feeling for the violence that was imposed on Muslim groups by Crusader's It was not unusual to see Christian travelers to get targeted and even killed on their travels. In the worst cases roadside, highwaymen killed traveling groups of hundreds. In the following decades, this violence escalated. Then some one was able to take action that would provide protection to pilgrims who were making their way. This man identified as Hugues de Payens, a French knight who was in 1119, a petitioner to the leaders of Jerusalem for their consent to create an entirely new society. The vision of De Payens was an order of monastic, religious organization, and a defiant group of knights that were to swear to offer protection for pilgrims. In 1120, his request was granted and the new group was referred to as The Knights Templar, was formed.

The name is derived from their headquarters. This new group was given an wings of the palace royal which was situated on top of Temple Mount, located within the mosque, which was taken over by the city's defenders were hiding prior to being executed. Some people thought it was odd to provide young people with this privileged piece real property. It was the beginning of many mysteries about knights Templar.

In the beginning, the group was able to meet one of the biggest needs of the newly established Christian governance within the Holy Land. Alongside other Monastic orders and other monastic orders, the Templars evolved into a temporary standing army. Despite their diverse ethnic backgrounds, kings of Jerusalem could finally show a professional, organized military force. It's no surprise that their ranks increased rapidly, and their significance was recognized quickly.

Along with the increase in number and power, the Templars saw a rise in power and wealth. In the beginning, the group was made up of nine knights with a lack of funds and an reliance on contributions from strong Christian rulers. In fact, the official name of their group was 'Poor Knights Christ as well as The Temple of Solomon.' To further stress the image of poverty on people around the globe, they chosen the symbol of two knights on a single horse, an iconic representation of the Templar's insufferable. However, this insufficiency was not sustained for long.

The Knights Templar had connections to important places. Through these friendships they swiftly moved up in the ranks of knights of the monastic order within the Holy Land. Members of the highest rank of the church rushed to praise them and eventually resulted in an official, formal approval by the Vatican. In this way, the Knights Templar were more than just a localized military organization. They earned a name and were a well-known name across in the Christian world. Then, the public was inspired to support the Templars. From all over Europe the people began to give funds, land, businesses and even relatives to Knights Templar. A powerful aristocratic clan sent one of their male members in their Holy Lands with the intent to be a member of the Templars. As the group's wealth increased and they were granted a second advantage when a papal decision called Omne Datum Optimum allowed them to be exempt from local laws of nations. The Templars, and the Templars all by themselves, it was believed-- could travel across any border, and not be subject to local taxes and were not subject to any authority aside from the pope and God. Within two decades, the knights the top of Temple Mount had become one of the richest and most powerful groups of their kind in the world.

Through the following years over the next few years, the Templars increased in importance and became crucial for the power balance in the Near East. In the fight against the famous Saladin and using the military's expertise and experience to continue their fight for the control of their territory in the Holy Land. While the victories in the military may have been vital for those living within the close proximity of Jerusalem but it was the increasing prosperity of the order that will be felt more throughout Europe. After the papal endorsements the coffers of the Knights Templar were overflowing. One of the most significant sources of revenue was when nobles and aristocrats entrusted their assets under the care by the Templars. If a nobleman wished to decide that they would "do their duty and participate in the Crusades and the Crusades, he could hand the transfer of his land and business to the Templars who would then manage the company in the absence of. They would receive a cut in exchange and the nobleman could be sure that his property would be given treatment and attention during the absence of him, and would be returned to him after leaving his home in the Holy Land. With the help of a myriad of revenue streams and sources, the Templars were able to create one of the biggest institutions of the medieval period. The bank was run by was the Knights Templar.

In the years that followed the Templars' expansion The vast majority of recruits were not assigned posts in the military, but to administrative roles. The reason was straightforward. There was a massive trend for a lot of people to travel across in the Holy Lands. The majority of these were wealthy Aristocrats who didn't want to carry their wealth around with their belongings because the land was usually populated by bandits. Today, they could travel around with only a small amount of money, and depend upon the Templars to assist them. It was believed that the Templars were a branch in all major cities. The money that was deposited at one of these offices would give the person an official letter that outlined the amount of money which was provided. When the person had reached Jerusalem the person could go to an additional branch at the Templars office to withdraw the money. This was an in many ways the prelude to modern banking system and the emergence of what is often called the first truly global group.

In barely a few years in any way in a short period of time, the Knights Templar were transformed from a small group of nine knights in need into one of the largest organizations around the globe. They were wealthy in many kinds. They took the grants they received as well as the profits they made and invested in lots across Europe as well as the Middle East. They constructed vineyards and farms and established businesses that earned them more money. They built cathedrals, castles and fortifications across Europe in as far away from their initial territories as was possible and with Templar forts being discovered further west than Portugal. They exported, imported manufactured, farmed banked, and even owned the fleet they owned of vessels which sailed across the Mediterranean. At one time they controlled the whole islands of Cyprus.

The Knights Templar increased in influential, other countries began to be aware. The initial Templars were a fervent group of knights, who were sworn to defend the poor pilgrims traveling through their journey to the Holy Land. At the close of the 12th century they had become one of the largest organisations on earth. They were not bound by local laws, not even in countries like France, Britain, and Germany. Only submitting to the pope and those who were envious of their Vatican began to look at those who were a part of the Templars as suspicious.

It's not uncommon to hear some of the theories about the Freemasons' ability to interact with the international banking world. Many have labeled the existence of big banks as a cabal of international origin and as the cause of many (seemingly disconnected) global incidents. In this sense it's not difficult to find parallels between these notions of the Freemasons and the banking practices of The Knights Templar. Although many make use of the (often fragile) relationship between Freemasons and the worldwide banking community as a defiant method, it is also reminiscent of antiquated suspicions about the Templars.

In the books on history it's not unusual to see people label those who were Knights Templar of the late 12th Century as arrogant. It's not difficult to imagine the reasons why they could be. In just 100 years, they had grown from humble beginnings to become a major global player. The first military commanders of the organization had long since passed and died, some in battle, others from natural reasons. The man who was in the charge as the Grand Master de Ridfort, was not liked by the high-ranking officials and nobles. They saw his company and the man who was in charge as arrogant.

Additionally to this, the power balance within The balance of power in Holy Land was beginning to tilt. Although the Crusaders had seized Jerusalem several decades ago but their hold over the region was beginning to be loosened. Saladin was an unprodigal commander who succeeded in securing control over several important places in the Levant. The Templars were once a crucial representation of Christian military power, became affected by the latest shortcomings. When Saladin's army achieved popularity, many began to feel resentment towards those who were Templars for their inability to retain control over this Holy Land. In the event that Saladin conquered Jerusalem in 1187 the city became a simple stick to defeat the Templars. The fact that the land remaining by Christians in the region, a tiny strip of land along the coast - was held by the Templars was an additional issue. People accused the Templars of protecting their own interests and not the interests of Christianity.

In the next century it was clear that power had shifted within the region. In 1296 in the year 1296, in 1296, the Holy Land was considered completely lost. Muslim rulers from Egypt had invaded from the south, and had helped in the complete removal of Christian influence out of the region. The Templars responded by shifting their main activities away from Levant and instead operating through their holdings in Cyprus. In Europe the rumblings of a second Crusade were heard, and the Templars focused on their business empires instead.

However, their adversaries did not forget. One of the most significant of the Templars enemies was Philip IV, the King of France, Philip IV. Philip had many reasons to dislike the order. Not only did he dislike their influence, and their immunity from local law, but also he found extremely dependent on the Templars. Desiring to continue his costly battles in the name of Edward I of England (rather than taking on an actual Crusade) He was envious of the prosperity that was the Knights Templar and wished to create his own. In Europe, He was fighting his own Holy Roman Empire (in modern times Germany) and also had an uneasy relationship between himself and the Vatican. Philip found himself in a challenging situation and the wealth of the Templars appeared to be the obvious to be a target.

Philip's fortunes changed following two significant events. The first was that his King England was killed. The replacement would be Edward II, who was weaker and less formidable opponent. In addition, a change of popes saw the former Holy See being replaced by a person more inclined to show Philip with respect The Frenchman Clement V. Clement V.

Initial reports indicated that the pope's election would be the start of the beginning of a new Crusade. It was not unusual for popes who were in the process of becoming popes to announce their plans to retake Jerusalem and, as it was announced that Pope Clement V ascended the Throne of Peter and they Knights Templar wondered whether a new crusade would mean the chance to go back in Jerusalem and the Holy Lands and retake their position of power and wealth as both had been declining since leaving the Levant. Enthusiastic to hear the thoughts from the newly elected pope the Templars sent their grandmaster to France to in the country where Clement was in residence.

The Grandmaster of Templars, Jacques de Molay was an old man. He came to France with a set of schemes and plans that the Templars created to help retake Jerusalem. He was welcomed with good intentions, humour and was welcomed. However, it wasn't to end there. In tandem, Philp and Clement had been plotting to bring down the Knights Templar. The 13th of October 1307, authorities launched an attack on the Templars and placed every Templar of the Templars in France on the run. Based on legends, this pivotal date fell on a Friday and the initial reason for why this date could be considered to be unlucky.

The arrests were more than significant by them. The Templars who were detained were tortured and punishment. Within those French cells, authorities seized confessions and admissions. Evidently, the Templars were now a depraved institution, plagued by worship of false gods and practices that were not christian and a lot of infractions. These confessions, which were not authentically obtained, were proclaimed as proof to this Templars' guilt. They were used as a guideline to dismantle the international organization of Knights Templar.

The battle in the fight against Templars within France was swift and brutal. However, it wasn't global. Although the pope issued a papal order to ban members of the Knights Templar, other rules weren't as quick to take action. In England For instance the new the King Edward II refrained from acting. Instead of arresting every Templars that he could He wrote to the Vatican to request the innocence of the order. After the pope responded by a decree that reiterated that decision Edward could not choose other than to take action and In January of 1308, he issued an arrest warrant in the case of those who were Templars located in England. Between the two acts however, residents of this order were given ample time to create a shortage of. Along with them was a large portion of their wealth not just precious metals and jewelry however, their detailed record of their activities as well.

In this way, the organization that was the Knights Templar was deemed illegal immediately. In the course of the French King toured all the Templar property and properties taking their wealth and assets for himself The group's global conglomerate was smashed up. With the members being officially labeled as heathens who worshiped devils It was no longer economically viable to as a member of the group. The Templars who were not snatched or tortured and then killed were forced to hiding. Because of the maneuvering by the government and the resulting pressure, this group had to transform into an underground society.

However, now after the Knights Templar were forced underground, where did they go? One of the only locations they could have left was Scotland. Scotland as well as a lot of other countries in Europe was in a tense political situation. Discordant with England as well as other European countries, they were exiled from the international community. The pressure of the English crown isolated from the Scottish royal family from Europe as well as the power from the pontiff. When the rest of Europe was busy hunting down the Templars while the Scottish didn't even issue an order to arrest them. They took care to hide themselves amid the turmoil It is believed that many of the Knights Templar took what they could from their wealth and traveled northwards to Scotland.

For certain people this is the point at which the theories regarding what constitutes the Knights Templar really begin to split. This is the point that there's a significant gap between the known history of the organization and those that seem to veer far off the track. Although we don't have the space to dive into the full depth of the darker aspect of the Templars the vast array of possibilities will give us a foundation which will aid in our understanding of the Freemasons.

A lot of focus on the present moment has been focused on the character of Templars wealth. While some people prefer to think of the wealth solely in financial terms however, some have suggested there was something much more fascinating being hidden in the Templars. What, they ask, did a tiny group of knights from a poor background gain power so quickly? How did they obtain such legal protection from church? The answer is said to be that it extends all the way all the way to Temple Mount. It is suggested that the Templars initial home in Jerusalem was much beyond the administrative headquarters. After being given the offices located in the building at the holy site, The Templars were digging. When they were digging they discovered... some thing. The precise kind of thing they might have discovered is as debated as the notion of whether they actually found anything. The discovery has been described as anything from the statue of Baphomet that was infused with dark magic power as well as an Ark of the Covenant (in which were stored the original tablets containing The Ten Commandments), or even the Holy Grail. The very nature of this latter item is argued to be anything from an ordinary cup used in the Last Supper, to being an extensive record of the lineage of mortal Jesus Christ, the family which he had on earth and his descendants up to present. Each of these items is regarded as the key to the Templars strength and for why they were capable of achieving the position they did in such a short time.

Finding out the circumstances surrounding the Knights Templarbut also the secrets they kept and what secrets they kept, has consumed the lives of many a historian. What is the best way to connect with the Freemasons? To understand this we must learn more regarding the Knights Templar and then look forward several years to the current state of England during the 14th Century.

Chapter 2: The Origins Of Freemasonry

"The carpenter extends the line and then draws the line using the pencil. He creates it using planes and marks it using the Compass. He molds it into the image of man, and he reveals the manly beauty living in a home." The text is Isaiah 44:13

The distinctive and diverse art of stonemasonry has existed since the beginning of civilisation, and particularly during those during the Neolithic Revolution of 10,000 BCE which saw people learn to manage both animals as well as land. In the wake of the groundbreaking finding of burning, early humans started to develop the first collection of tools for building. The first innovations in construction technology came later. The process of heating limestone in mortars by the aid of water, created an corrosive white substance called "quicklime." The well-balanced mixture of sand, cement and crushed limestone was created plaster, which was then used to cover ceilings, walls and other surfaces to give smooth and strong appearance.

Stonemasonry has provided mankind with all its human-made marvels. Stonemasons, also referred to in the broader sense of "stone-cutters," helped design burial mounds, the classic tall pyramids of Egypt and the magnificent step pyramids that were used to build the step pyramids used in Incan, Mayan, and other Mesoamerican communities. Stone-cutters from the thriving community also played an important role in the creation of the first cathedrals, temples and castles across the globe, as being the famous monuments in Cuzco's Ican Wall, Stonehenge, and the Easter Island Statues, among numerous others.

They were also the first to pioneer their field, calligraphy. They are the very first people to write messages onto stone, which was the first medium for human communication. Egyptian stonemasons are believed to have invented an alphabetic language known as hieroglyphics an alphabet of symbols written across stone tablets and walls to communicate messages to each another, and also their future descendants. As the development of society continued across the globe, people began writing on stones, immortalizing the writing and various literary works.

Stonemasons were part of guilds which were basically associations of similar-minded merchants and craftsmen who were engaged in the same trade. The initial guilds contained people from a particular town at first, but in the course in the Middle Ages, when the demand for skilled stonemasons increased and the guilds grew, they grew. Leaders and nobles of wealth from distant and near regions began to call upon masons to assist for a myriad different construction tasks. This led to a number of people who considered the stonemasons to be marginalized members of society because they led erratic, nomadic lives, moving from one location to the next in pursuit of the scent of work.

The stonemasons were divided into three classes: masters and apprentices as well as the master stonemasons. Apprentices were aspiring and novice craftsmen who were indentured apprentices and laborers to their masters for specific one-on-one education. The journeymen had completed their training and, as the name implies they accompanied their masters for assistance on construction projects in remote cities. Master masons were the highest class of stonemasons. being awarded to the most educated and skilled of the craftsmen within the guild. The masters had the ultimate decision, and had full control over the construction sites, and all builders, carpenters and other craftsmen beneath him.

Stonemasons created a variety of tools to help them master their art of stonemasoning. Stonemasons first used stones that were abrasive to use as carving tools. The discovery of additional metals gave an opportunity to the invention of mallets, chisels, drills, hammers, and saws made of iron. A few of the widely employed stonemason tools was the punch hammer. It was a specialized hammer that had a small, multi-purpose head which made it simpler to form stone. Another tool that was adored was the masonic square as well as Compass that consisted of a drawing compass as well as an angle square merged. Following each work the guild would leave an e-card of some sort and a distinct symbol that was in the form, like artists did with create their masterpieces.

The medieval guilds quickly developed communities, each with a "mystery" that was their very own. Masonic secrets were organized as schools of esoteric research that focused on the methodological and philosophical concepts that underlie the creation of these stunning and intricately framed towers as well as structures. Similar to the contemporary companies like Coca-Cola or Kentucky Fried Chicken, which are well-known for their commitment to draw an opaque veil over the hidden ingredients used in their recipes, the techniques of the stonemason trade were intended to last and be buried in the guild. Only master masons could hold the secrets of this trade.

The rising art of masonry took its way through the globe. The 10th century was when the new trend was introduced to England and, was led by King Athelstan who was known for his love for architecture. The masons of the country were eager to see the king to get advice on trade. To please his people the king brought together all the earls, dukes scholars, noblemen, and dukes from the country, and, together, came up with the following documents and notes which would be used as a foundation for masonic guidelines and an instruction manual for moral conduct and business practices that would be executed by master masons apprentices and journeymen as well.

In accordance with the provisions of the articles that a master mason must be honest, faithful and was able to use good judgment. According to masonic law, they were obliged to pay their employees equally and fairly. Apprentices had to go across the identical hoops in the screening process. the bribes of those who sought to gain access to the guild could be denied without hesitation. Master masons had to attend every meeting scheduled and could only be excused in case of a health issue. They were required to scrutinize each project carefully prior to approving the project and to ensure that the budget was used in a proper manner and resources.

Apprentices were only admitted in the event that they were able to complete the required seven years to the education of the trade. The majority of apprentices were young, sturdy, and in excellent physical condition as they believed that the disabled and sickly would slow their development. The same was true for those who were unable to meet the masonic standards were kicked out and replaced as soon as they could. The most important thing was that apprentices were required to keep the rap sheets in the same condition as their health certificates. The rapists, thieves, and murderers could not be found in society.

An uncompromising code of respect for each other and discipline was instilled throughout daily activities. Master masons were not allowed to inscrutablely stealing the projects of masters. The greedy masters who did not comply were required to pay an L10 fine (roughly 10600 dollars today). Masons were averse to criticism that was demeaning and gave only helpful advice to brothers who they disagreed with. The issue could be settled with respect and in a civil way. Master masons were accountable to maintain a sense of unity as well as integrity and professionalism within their guilds.

The early members were devout and God-fearing believers who pledged to honor and love their masters and their fellow brothers at all times. The members pledged to never speak any word of the guild's principles. They were forbidden from doing harm to others within their circle including the seemingly innocent act of sexing a brother's wifeto shocking physical hurt or violence. The group was expected to keep a strict yet harmonious atmosphere within their group, fuelled by love for one another and the desire to improve the art of. The meetings were scheduled frequently, with the permission of the monarch in power usually once a year and, at minimum, once every three years.

The poem's origin also provided some of the first mentions of the Sancti Quatuor Coronati, or in English it was"the "Four crowned martyrs." The term was the name that was given to two distinct, but equally courageous groups of Christians that were all sculptors artisans, and engravers of trade. The emperor had each group to make an exhibition of paintings of sculptures, murals as well as other idols, in his name. This meant that all representations of Christ were to be removed from all homes in the country and replaced with an unholy image of the Emperor. Every single one of the people who were enlisted declined, and as a result, every one of them was condemned to their grisly death.

It was in 1861 that Matthew Cooke published another version of the Freemasonry the story of its beginnings. The only difference was that instead of using scrolls, the book is printed on Vellum an exclusive parchment made of the calfskin. The rise of this brand new form of literature was to revive the Freemasonry interest in Britain. Cooke's manuscript provided a brief overview of the seven Liberal Sciences. There the "grammar," the primary foundation of all sciences. It provides an order to writing and reading. The next step was "rhetoric," which trained the person to communicate in a manner that is eloquent and diction. The third is "dialectic," otherwise referred to as "logic," which gave an individual the ability to differentiate between the truth and lies. Fourth one was "arithmetic," which was the fundamental structure for the study of numbers. The fifth is "geometry," the art of measuring and weighing, an essential part of the creation of everything. After that, followed "music," and lastly, "astronomy."

The second half of the document provided a different view of the origins of Freemasonry. The manuscript said that the geniuses responsible for the greatest science were descendants of Lamech the 6th line descendant of Cain most famous for the story in the Bible about his brother's death. Jabal Lamech's oldest son was recognized as the one who discovered geometrical concepts and masonry. He was among the most highly regarded carpenters of his day demonstrated his remarkable capabilities by building hundreds of homes to the community. He soon rose to the top of the ladder and earned his title as master mason working as a direct subordinate to Cain himself. Cain and his brother were said to have constructed Enoch situated just east of Eden It was the first city ever built in the world.

Jubal Lamech's son, who was the second discovered music and created one of the first instruments such as the kinnor which was an old Harp, as well as the uggab, which was a wood flute. Tubal-cain was half-brother of Jabal and Jubal was the first to discover metalworking the study of metals and is believed to be the first blacksmith in the world. The daughter of Lamech Naamah created weaving as a craft by laying the foundations of the art of making clothes.

The skilled siblings were able to prophesy about the coming end of the world and believed that one day it would be swallowed up by water, fire or some other natural catastrophe. They determined to leave their knowledge to the generations to come and engrave their revered knowledge of the seven sciences by constructing a pair stone pillars. One was made to be insinkable and the other in a flame-proofed. After centuries of the catastrophic flood that led to rising another bigwig from the Bible, Noah, the pillars were able to be sunk onto the ocean floor. One of them was found by Hermes who was a revered philosopher and the founder of Hermeticism. The other was pulled from the sea by Pythagoras and would later become a prominent name in the field of mathematics.

The 7 sciences were handed over to Nimrod as the architect in charge for Babel. Tower of Babel. Lateron, the knowledge found its way to Abraham who would later on time become one of the most revered patriarchs in Judaism. From Abraham the knowledge-based river flowed to Euclid and the Egyptians and the Israelites and then the rest is history.

Incredibly enough, one of the most well-known stories of the origin originates from a mixture of tradition and speculation rather than factual evidence, and yet it is accepted by modern Freemasons all the same. The story is further back in history and at the very least, a millennium prior to when Christ was believed to be born. Solomon of Israel was King Solomon of Israel had planned to build an amazing site of worship in Jerusalem however, to complete the ambitious goal He had to look to Hiram, the king of Tyre for assistance. In addition to a list of the materials Solomon was lacking, he sought an expert craftsman. The skilled craftsperson, Solomon said, was "cunning enough be able to do work with gold and also in silver, in brass, as well as in iron, as well as in purple, blue and crimson."

After some consideration after some reflection, The King of Tyre was willing to accept Solomon's request for wine, corn and oil. In return, he offered Solomon heaps of cedar wood freshly cut out of Lebanese forests, as well as his most cherished craftsman. It was Hiram Abiff who was his father was a dead metalworker and the "widow belonging to the clan of Naphtali." Abiff stepped into the role confidently and with an unstoppable determination. He quickly proved his skill in masonry and was eventually elevated as Master Mason by

Solomon and was tasked with the enthralling construction of the now famous Temple of Solomon. More than 85,000 workers were assembled to work on the project under Abiff's direction, one which took seven years to finish. Anyone who worked for all seven years of their lives from beginning to end and were crowned Master Masons at the conclusion of the undertaking.

Chapter 3: Wolfgang Sauber's Drawing Of A

Stained Glass Representation Of Hiram Abiff

It is believed that the Temple of Solomon would be the most magnificent and revered of the temples, as it would house the first tablets of the "Ten Commandments." The blueprints of the advanced design and layout were said to have been given by Solomon by the sole and undisputed Almighty. This valuable knowledge was hidden in the shadows, and only accessible to one soul - Abiff.

A beautiful rendering from Solomon's Temple. Temple of Solomon

In the course of building, Abiff along with his men started to create a secret culture. The secret code was devised and only made available to graduates of apprentices and journeymen to give them an award of achievement. To greet each other, Abiff and his workers invented the first version of handshakes that were secret and signs.

At the point of completion Three of Hiram's followers started to sweat with apprehension.

The uneasy apprentices thought the whole incident was nothing more than a ruse for free labordevised by Abiff. Incredulous of their own conclusions they rushed to Hiram in the first place and started to ask Hiram about that secret phrase or, at a minimum an inkling of the divine wisdom that which the Master Mason claimed to possess.

Unnerved but not discouraged, Hiram brushed them off and urged the men to be gentle. This only reinforced their misguided notions. They began to adhere to the notion of the password being the sole thing that stood between them and their guild's secret wisdom, a treasure chest of wisdom believed to give them supernatural abilities.

Then they realized that they could stay up all night. They analyzed Abiff's schedule to the letter. The master mason was known for his habit of leaving the temple each day at noon to pray. In this regard, the trio strategically placed themselves around the temple, squatting behind each of the three exits. Abiff tried to escape through the east entrance however, he was immediately surrounded. The first mason who was rogue demanded Abiff about the password but the calm master hardly glanced at them and was unable to comply. When Abiff was able to turn to his right and retreated, the mason in rage picked an icy stone close to him, and then cut the master in the neck.

He clenched his throat. Abiff was able to free himself and then stumbled toward the south-facing door and the second man stood waiting. Again, Abiff rebuffed the second mason's plea. As Abiff was swaying away from the mason, he used a masonic square on his head and struck him across the face.

A lost Abiff fell over the pool of blood of himself, and began to walk towards the west door. Again, Abiff, just a hair's distance from his death was unable to reveal the password. The last mason was thrown into a anger rage and struck the fatal blow using the sharp edge of the chalice made of stone. Abiff fell to the ground. The master was bleeding out his lungs, he yelled, "Who will help the widow's son?"

A few years later, Abiff's last words were his Freemasons' "universal cry for assistance." From the time Abiff died, Hiram Abiff was embraced as the embodiment for the very first "free mason" the builder that was adamant about the freedom to be free in all aspects such as religion, speech and character, and so on. In the words of Abiff the term "free mason" means that an abbot or Freemason is a constructor as well as freed from the constraints imposed by the shackles of slavery or civic obligations. As with Abiff, the Freemason is expected to fend off a trio of adversaries - ignorance hatred, and despotism.

Another theory ties the Freemasons' ancestry to a totally different mythological society. The year 1120 was the time that Christian knights took over the city Jerusalem and began an initial phase of Crusades. Routes for pilgrimages taken by people who came from cities nearby became filled with murderers, robbers and other criminals. A group of knights gathered to tackle the ever-growing problem. In a monastic vow and a trip towards The Holy Land, where they began to defend innocent pilgrims. The happy king honored them with their own spot on the Temple Mount. They soon made an identity as they were known as the Knights Templar.

The Seal of the Knights Templar

The place of worship was known in the form of the "Al-aqsa Mosque" that was constructed on top of the remains of the Temple of Solomon. There were rumors of knights digging up the rubble and removing the dirt in the hope of finding a lost treasure called "Solomon's gold." Not only did the knights have success in locating Solomon's riches over the course of nine years, but they also were reported to have discovered the legend of the Holy Grail, as well as sacred parchments written by the writers of the Dead Sea Scrolls. The parchment was among the most valuable of all the treasures, since it was filled with instructions that allowed the direct communicating between God and mankind.

The knights who were now armed with incredible treasures, returned back to Europe and joined with the Catholic Church. There they were one of the most powerful classes of Medieval Europe. A large portion of their earnings were donated to charities. Knights used a band of stonemasons to construct monasteries, chambers and places of worship across Europe which included the striking domed Temple Church in London. They also are believed to have changed the way banks operate in the form of minting coins, and also implementing the first security system. Stonemasons were apprentices to knights, whom, at a later date were gifted with the secrets of the scrolls. These ancient rituals were later an integral part of Freemasonry's tradition.

The public began to become cynical about the knights' community who regularly held private gatherings and elaborate rituals that were kept from the spotlight. It wasn't for long before the practices that were practiced by those of the Knights Templar were deemed "un-Christian" by the people around them. One Friday , 13th June 1307 under the orders of the French King, troops swarmed into Templar headquarters with the intention of cuffing the knights, and confiscating their wealth and possessions. The knights who were disgraced were accused with heresy, blasphemy and the cult of satanic deities.

In 1312 the society was officially prohibited in 1312 by Pope Francis. The no longer shrewd knights, who were capable of escaping execution were able to escape to Scotland and were scattered across Europe. Some say that others were still in England in the hope of reviving the order under a different name around 100 years or so afterward: Freemasons.

Modern historians have discovered new evidence linking with Freemasons and The Knights Templar through the specific geometrical carvings within the walls at the Scottish Rosslyn Chapel. The charming, white-stone chapel is a favourite spot for thriller writers through the centuries, was hidden back behind a curtain of lush trees and greenery in the rural countryside. The creator of the chapel is William Sinclair, an earl and lineage holder from Norman knights. This very chapel, some historians claim, was one of the places where the new Templar-turned-Freemasons found refuge.

Anne Burgess' picture of the chapel.

The picture is Jeremy A.'s photograph from the inside of the church

It is believed that the Sinclair family was believed to have strong ties with European Freemasons. They were heirs to the Grand Master of Freemasonry in Scotland and were conferred this title on them in the beginning of the 17th century. Many claim that the title was conferred upon them earlier at a date.

Once they have established this, the claim is yet to be proved, since the blueprints that were originally used for the building for Rosslyn Chapel have been destroyed by fire. Rosslyn Chapel have been erased through a massive fire.

Schaw, Scotland, and Suppression

"Ideals are as stars. They will not let you succeed in touching them by hand however, just like the sea-faring man pick them as your guides and by following them, you can reach your goals." Carl Schurz

Demand for the masonry trade was expected to increase to a new high during the early 15th century. Due to the increasing numbers of Freemasons internal conflicts and discord were increasing which led to head-butting and split-off factions. Some of these fractured groups were seen as so chaotic and difficult to manage that local authorities started to issue laws restricting their activities with the aim to limit the growth of these groups.

However, the market for masons increased in size with the passage of the passing of time. In 1475, masons from Edinburgh, Scotland were in the process of being granted a charter. Edinburgh, Scotland were presented with the "Seal of Cause" a charter from the past that was given to them by their authorities. The charter brought together masons, carpenters as well as coopers (cask and barrel makers) into one "incorporated" group. The new entity, referred to by the name of an "English trade guild" was joined together through the new rules and regulations imposed by the state. The Freemasons for the first time were an official trade, joining the ranks of other trades that were incorporated, such as the Baxters bread-makers, also known as bakers and the Hammermen metal artisans and metallurgy specialists and the Wabsters who are the needle-pushers and weavers of the town.

The masons of Edinburgh developed a more complicated system known as "lodges," which were fundamentally guilds, which were divided into different classes, with the ones at the crown ruling over the classes below them. After years of urging the establishment of lodges of masonic order authorities finally conceded at the end of 1491. The years that followed Freemasonry continued to spread throughout Europe and lodges were established all over the world. In 1535 in

1535, the Freemason phenomenon had spread all the way to France. There were at most two confirmed Scottish lodges of masonic worship within the city of Lyon as well as Paris.

The Freemason expansion ended abruptly at the time in the Protestant Reformation in the early 16th century. The religious, political, and cultural turmoil had been initiated by complaints and grievances against the corrupt Catholic Church. The Church was slammed and publicly criticized for simony which was a type of under-the-table fee paid by Catholic authorities to allow entry into or an upgrade of the government of religion. The worst part was the selling of indulgences, which that one could be charged for tickets to Heaven.

This Protestant movement was especially prevalent in central and northern Europe which was which is where rebels such as Martin Luther, John Calvin along with the king Henry VIII of England took an oath against Catholics hoping to having their power distributed to those who had created their own particular kind of Christian faith. Although he was not the one who was a theologian and his resentment against the

Vatican was grounded in concerns of a secular nature about succession Henry VIII attempted to destroy the foundations and rub away all evidence to Catholicism in England and even demanded the removal of all monasteries in the nation in the late 1530s. The monasteries had become the focus of the ominous the king's fury, as they were believed to be in the midst of a conspiracy and were still toying with the papacy. It was a good timing because at this point the substantial inheritance that had received from his father was towards its final leg. Thomas Cromwell, the king's Chief Minister, only increased the monarch's phobia by saying that the proceeds from monasteries were channeled back to the Vatican at the close of every year.

Luther

Calvin

Henry VIII

Cromwell

Although the incident is currently called"the "Dissolution of monasteries" many religious establishments were destroyed such as abbeys, nunneries and chapels, cathedrals as well as other locations that were used for Catholic worship. Cromwell who was as the head of the nation's operations in the field of religion and had ordered a massive investigation of these institutions. his troops ripped down their doors and marched into these spaces, wearing royal warrants and shiny weapons in their belts. They searched every corner looking for signs of disobedience to the reformed Church of England. Many believed that the documents made by these raids which were led by Cromwell's right-hand men, were manipulated to create false reports that they believed to satisfy their superior's almost impossible amount of work.

The protests of the shrinking Catholic public were ignored. In the month of March 1536 Parliament took action by enacting a controversial act calling for the closing and confiscation of property from all monastery and Catholic institutions with annual revenues below L200 ($46,108 USD) that took effect immediately. More than 300 of these small Catholic establishments met the criteria and the vast majority were demolished. Some 67 of these institutions were pardoned by the king, however they had to pay huge taxes in order to maintain their doors and, on average, amount to around a whole year's worth of revenue.

Just a few years after that, authorities began to examine the Freemasons. They, after all depended on Catholic-funded projects to earn the bulk of their earnings. They could have taken an unavoidable hit due to the deportation of their long-time employers, but they managed to remain afloat.

In 1548, one year following the death of King Henry VIII and in 1548, the Bill of Conspiracies of Victuallers and Craftsmen was approved. The decree was a call for the dissolution of all guilds of craft in 1548, and made their monopolies null. Fortunately for craftsmen that ban was repealed within a year, due to the fact that the absence of the masonic industry affected the market. From that point onward and through the following century English government officials along with nobles, and other wealthy people, revived the practice of hiring masons to tackle difficult construction projects. Although their right to trade was restored however, religious masonic festivals such as Saint's day Parades, were prohibited.

Scottish Masonic lodges were administered by two officials chosen by the monarch. They were Warden General and Chief Master of Work of the Scottish Crown. The one on the left was the most prominent post, which was given to an official who was responsible for all construction, repairs and related matters for the palaces and other properties of the monarch.

As the 16th century came to an end one man by his name William Schaw bore both titles. William Schaw, who was born 1550 in Broich which is now Arngomery located in Stirlingshire, Scotland, is widely regarded as being among the pioneers of contemporary Freemasonry. The Schaw family has always been very familiar to the Scottish crown as they took care of the wine cellar at royal residence for many generations. In 1580 the Schaw name was in the news after William's dad, John is accused of the murder of nearby nobleman's servant. John then eluded the court dates, resulting in the seizing from Schaw's estate. Schaw property until the matter was finally solved.

Schaw

Young William was able to free himself from the scandal surrounding his father determined to create his own career path that was his own. At first, he was a court page of Edinburgh followed by an official in members of the entourage Esme Stuart, Duke of Lennox. The Anglican-born William then took an oath of loyalty in the Church of England, cementing his connection to the crown. The following year, in the month of April 1581, the 31-year-old William was recognized for his loyalty to the country and was presented with land in Kippen the village of the western part of Stirlingshire.

On the 21st of December, 1583 On the 21st of December 1583, the King James VI of Scotland (the future King James I of England) named William as the Chief Master of the Works of Scotland, a title that was secured through an advance payment of L166 ($38,270 USD) salary for the month prior. William's initial official duty was to organize the lodges of masonic worship. After putting in his thinking caps the masonic master began his work in a flash. In 1598, while in the meeting of the masters of the masonic in Southeastern Scotland, William unveiled his first version of "Schaw's Statutes."

The first statutes defined new titles, like deacons and wardens, and laid out a more central the governing body. The duties were clarified and handed out to everyone at every level. In addition, the statutes outlined the penalties for those who was not up to standards, and people who had a history of unsafe work practices. William advised masons to remain "true to each other and to live in a way that is wholesome in the fellowship of the sworn brethren to The Craft."

A revision of statutes released one year later. The raging over power in the swollen lodges resulted in the creation that of Edinburgh Chapter. Edinburgh Chapter as the "first and primary lodge" and the Kilwinning lodge as Kilwinning being the second position. Perhaps most important, the amended statutes were the very first document that made reference in"esoteric knowledge," or "esoteric knowledge" that was stored within the midst of Freemasonry. Additionally, lodges were required to keep meticulous reports, also called "meeting minutes" and meet regularly for annual meetings.

In the late 16th to 17th century the number of scholars, artists and other speculative Freemasons joined the fray. All sorts of people were caught up in the mystery of the craft as they became fascinated by the intricate designs and structures the stone-cutters made. In the Age of Reason, otherwise called the European Enlightenment of the 18th century, also led to an increase of Freemasonry membership. Naturally it wasn't everyone happy with the increase in membership. Although the Enlightenment promoted revolutionary ideas that were closely resembling Freemason ideals, lodges were viewed as secret society. People who disapproved of the persecution of their religion were also believed to have left to lodges.

In the late summer of 1717 the very first grand lodge - the governance body for an organization of fraternity or guild in a particular region was established in England. It was called the Premier Grand Lodge of England which is now called"the "Grand Lodge of England" is still the oldest lodge of masonic in existence. In 1720, a grand lodge was created in Ireland. The following year that, all grand lodges were able to only be recognized by warrants that were approved by the government.

A 19th century painting of the inside of the Grand Lodge. Grand Lodge

In 1723 in 1723, an Presbyterian priest, Father James Anderson, published The Constitutions of the Free-Masons. The document provided a complete step-by step procedure that was applicable to the Premier Grand Lodge of England and every lodge in London and Westminster that were under the jurisdiction of its members. The constitution, in the form of documents of the old masonic manuscripts which are also referred to as "Gothic Constitutions" it was also the first to describe the history that was told by Hiram Abiff. The constitution also contained an complex diagram of the Freemasonry levels.

This is the title page for Anderson's Constitutions

In 1735, Scottish lodges met to discuss the formation of their grand lodge. The 33 members present chose William Sinclair of Rosslyn as the first Grand Master Mason and officially created the Grand Lodge in the year 1736. The headquarters of these new lodges, and any other bases to come will share a layout that was shared with that of the Temple of Solomon.

As the idea of grand lodges started to take hold as the popularity of grand lodges grew, the number of lodges masonic throughout the continent grew. In 1725, annual meeting minutes revealed that the movement was spreading to the south, revealing at least 10 lodges located in Salford in Great Manchester in Northwest England and South Wales. After the establishment of the Scottish Grand Lodge however, the sky above the masons began to darken.

A group of master masons and wardens members of an Irish lodge were stopped by the door of the national grand lodge due to the warrants they issued were declared ineligible. The angry masons cultivated their new resentment against grand lodges and splits within guilds increased by a third. In fear of reprisal and the intrusion of outsiders, grand lodges across Europe have tightened security measures by introducing new rules for passwords that require more intricate handshakes. The new security measures have just sparked more discord between the leaders of grand lodges, causing a deeper gap within the community.

Despite the growing divisions the lodges continued to experience constant growth. The 18th century was the time when they began to grow The Freemasons also reached a milestone by obtaining the first international charter the approval of an lodge located in Aleppo, Syria. At this time there was a significant number of Freemasons were part of armies that were sent abroad. These Freemasons were given "traveling charters" which permitted them to spread their branches into the nations they worked.

Chapter 4: The Core Of The Craft

A 18th century French illustration of the process of Masonic ceremony of initiation.

"Masonry is among the most beautiful and ideal institutions ever created to promote happiness and for humanity's general welfare by generating it in all its forms universal kindness and brotherly affection." Prince Augustus Frederick, Duke of Sussex

In a homage to traditional construction The Scottish Freemasons had three "Blue Lodge" degrees.

One of them was called the "Entered Apprentice," which was a symbol of the rebirth of the person who was aspiring to become a candidate. The student was dressed in pitch-blackand had to follow a maze of darkness by his teacher in order to find the light or the sacred "knowledge" in the middle of the road. The newcomers would have only had access to what was made public about the history of Freemasonry. A brief introduction was provided through a Junior Warden that gave them a broad knowledge of the actual meaning and significance of The Temple of Solomon.

"Fellowcraft Degree" followed "Fellowcraft Degree" was the next step. At this point the previous apprentices were already finished with the initial lectures and instruction. Under the guidance by a senior Warden they explored the history of the society, and were taught about the everyday life and struggles of medieval and biblical craftsmen. At the time of this time, they would have been given to discuss the building and completion of Solomon's Temple.

The final degree was "Master Mason." Masters were well-versed with the lessons of his previous degrees. The new courses they taught were centered around the epic story of Hiram Abiff and the way he gave his life to the cause of society. They were also provided with the entire scope of the ideology that shaped freemasonry. In general the title of Master Mason was the highest of all degrees. In a similar spirit to master's degrees from collegiate universities Master Masons can choose to pursue additional training. For those who want to satisfy an insatiable need for knowledge can turn to the two areas of Master Masonry - the Scottish and York Rites.

The first subbranch, comprised of the first 14 of the Scottish Rites was known as the "Lodge of Perfection." The classes in this subbranch include "Master Traveler,"" "Intendant of the Building,"" "Grand Master Architect,"" and "Grand Mason Elect." These qualifications were created to improve the master's sense of loyalty, duty as well as honesty and confidentiality. The curriculum also included self-protection and neighborly values that included the elimination of unclean and selfish thoughts as well as being impartial and fair in judging. In addition, a master learnt how to use the skills acquired and the resources acquired throughout his education to strengthen his relationship with God and also to endure through the midst of challenges.

This second branch was called"the "council on Princes from Jerusalem," which consisted of just two degrees -"the "Knight of the East," and the "Prince of Jerusalem." Similar to previous degrees, masters were provided with greater knowledge of the requirements to commit themselves towards the goal. Third subbranch known as the "Chapter of the Rose Croix," which included two degrees -"The "Knight of both the East as well as the West," and the "Knight of the Rose Croix." The lessons shifted towards the religious aspect, educating the masters about the importance of a commitment to God and the relationship that one must cherish above everything other relationships. The masters were also taught to make their hearts an altar to God but also to be open to accepting their fellow brothers who had different beliefs.

The last bracket was referred to in the "Consistory," which contained the final 14 degrees of the Scottish Rite. The titles included "Grand Pontiff,"" "Chief of the Tabernacle," "Prince of Mercy,"" as well as"Prince of Mercy," and the "Grand Inspector." Master of the past were put through a series of tests that tested their dedication to the cause and also the strength of their personal faith and the character of their.

The highest of heights was "Sublime prince of the royal Secret." At the final phase spirituality was able to overpower the mortal part of the master. They had the power to control all impure cravings and emotions effortlessly and had an unblinking moral compass and a rational.

The York Rite Graduation were another set of additional degrees accessible to master masons looking for to gain a deeper source of information. The first subbranches was known as the "Royal Arch" that comprised 4 levels, including"Mark," "Past," and "Most Excellent" Masters "Mark," "Past," and "Most Excellent" Masters as well as"the "Royal Arch." The virtues of work, charity and kindness were also taught to masters. They also took an education course in the historical background of Solomon's Temple.

The next subbranch of the "Cryptic Rite" comprises 4 degrees , including"Super-Excellent," "Royal, "Royal," "Select," "Super-Excellent," and "Thrice Illustrious" Masters. The masters here were given an extra-depth overview of the history of the temple as they dealt with events that occurred prior to and after the construction of the temple as well as the expulsion of Hebrews. The final group of subbranches was known as the "Chivalric Masonry" made up of the three final York degrees: the "Illustrious Order of the Red

Cross,"" The "Order of Malta" along with the "Order of the Temple." Although these names appear to honor other mystical brotherhoods, the concrete evidence for any link to those of the Freemasons or the Rosicrucians and any other fraternal organization is not yet confirmed.

There were five basic requirements required for Freemason applicants. First of all the society was only accepting solid, "unmutilated," free men. Only those with clean reports, excellent recommendations and a good reputation within society were thought of. With the exception of a few lodges in the modern era that include women in recent years including lodges like the Order of the Eastern Star Traditional lodges consisted of males only.

In addition, one needed to be a believer in a god and also a the possibility of life after death. The nature of the supreme being was not specified as a result of a reason. Freemasons have a fervent acceptance of Jewish, Muslim, Hindu and other non-Christian beliefs caused a lot of controversy in the past. It is no surprise that the atheists and pagans were thrown off.

The third requirement was that candidates had to be in stable financial status, and possess the complete and unaided capacity to sustain their families as well as themselves. This requirement was put in place in order to eliminate anyone who wanted to take advantage of the society to get financial assistance. It also highlighted the importance of putting God and family before the brotherhood.

Then, all applicants had to be over the age of 18. This was a requirement that varied from lodge to lodge, however, overall the minimum age for admission was 21. Finally, only those who joined by their "own libre will and consent" were allowed to join. Contrary to most brotherhoods Freemasons were not affluent. Freemasons didn't actively solicit members and, in keeping with their adherence to secrecy, they did not promote or promoted themselves. They relied on the word of mouth, which was evidently an effective method, because it allowed them to maintain the same growth rate over many centuries.

What really happens behind the rituals and initiations is not known to the public.

However, over time, many confirmed brothers have offered to shed light on the subject with brief descriptions of the procedure.

The candidates who are interested submitted petitions which were then sent to lodges that informed the society about the interest of the candidate. The lodge did some study on the candidate's background and a board session was scheduled to discuss as well as vote for the admission of the possible Freemason. After the candidate had been voted through, they were declared an "Entered Apprentice" and started their journey towards achieving the dazzling light that is"full Masonic light. "full Masonic light."

If an Freemason was elevated to the next level and was rewarded by having graduation ceremonies that had the same theme. Brothers were blindfolded by the "masonic hoodwink" prior to entering the Chamber of Reflection. They were guided through a sacred reenactment Hiram Abiff's death in the temple. They ended up receiving a token of"Masonic light. "Masonic Light."

After they were shown the light then the hoodwink was removed. The person who was hoodwinked was asked to stand before an altar and swear an vow. In a bible of their favorite scriptures in their hands, they took an oath to follow all rules and to keep the secrecy of the society throughout their lifetime. When the brother was committed to silence and masonic symbols, signals handshakes, other secrets of etiquette were exposed to him.

As mentioned previously that the guidelines of the society were formed through the writings of Gothic constitutions as well as"the so-called "Old Charges" that were manuscripts written during the transition from operating to speculational Freemasonry. The rules and regulations was condensed into an array of 25 "landmarks" written by The Dr. Albert Mackey, a physician and author in early in the nineteenth century. Mackey started with General Lodge Management. All lodges were divided into three degrees, and each lodge would be overseen by an Grand Master. Two Master Principals and Wardens were chosen to oversee and run all lodge meetings. The use of weapons of all kinds were allowed inside the lodges or conference facilities.

Visitors from outside and those who did not be able to pass an examination administered by the authorities were swiftly removed. Like always lodges were not allowed to interference in the operations of other lodges.

Mackey

An "Book of Law" was to be displayed in each lodge for quick access, as well as to safeguard the rights for all Freemasons. Individual rights of Freemasons were reiterated. They had the right to be represented in all meetings and also the right to visit and join with lodge members from other lodges. In addition each brother of any grade were required to display the ideals of respect, understanding and fairness not just to each other, but to all members of the society.

The primary goal for their Freemasons is in order to "make better men from excellent males." They tried to mould the character of a person by expanding their spiritual and moral perspectives. While doing so they wanted to help educate each other about personal responsibility and ethics, as well as how to integrate these concepts into their daily lives.

In addition to a inviolable moral code, Freemasons wanted to help their followers open their minds to the importance of social responsibility and charity and the capacity to stand with impartial and uninfluenced opinions on religion as well as politics and other controversies.

As the customs and culture of Freemasonry changed as did the society's manners and customs. The mention of politics, religion, or other personal matters in lodge gatherings were forbidden and could not be considered as the basis for the making of any decisions. Being seated in the East in the East without invitation was considered to be disrespectful since the seats were reserved for the masters with the highest rank members of lodge. Freemasons were forbidden to talk or discuss topics which were not agreed upon prior to the conferences. Participants were required to wear all the proper attire, including the black suit with gloves, gauntlet-cuffs and gloves lapel pins, and an embossed the apron. It was an ode to their stonemason ancestral ancestors.

A myriad of emblems have been revealed through the years, which were created to represent various Freemason factions. The Society of Freemasonry is recognized with a unique logo, an masonic square and compass with an enunciated "G" in the center. The square is believed to remind one to "square" your actions through morality, while the compass was a way to "circumscribe" the passions of one's life. The majority of Freemasons believe that the mystical "G" is a reference to "God." Some have offered "Gnostic" and "Geometry," as these are the fundamental elements of the Freemason life.

A photo of the logo on the grave of Mackey.

The range of masonic symbolism has progressively grown over time. The most recognizable symbols among the many can be"the "Eye of Providence" which is also known as "All-Seeing Eye." The image that was derived from other ancient civilizations, can be present in nearly every lodge across the globe in the present. The unblinking eye is a reference to an unnamed god who watches over the community and, as Mackey declared, is an "symbol of speed as well as strength as well as the sign of loyalty."

A earliest Masonic variant of the Eye of Providence

Eye of Providence Eye of Providence is located on the reverse of the Great Seal of the United States

Another common symbol can be found in the "Level and"Plumb." This tool for building was utilized to determine the level of horizontal, flat surfaces, was a symbol that human beings lived at"the "level that time." This was also thought of as a symbol of equality and balance and is further supported by the Freemason motto, "We all meet on the same level."

Bulls, Intervention, and the American Project

"Freemasonry is an organization designed to serve humanity." -- Andrew Jackson

Around the middle of the 18th century in the mid-18th century, in the mid-18th century, Roman Catholic Church declared all secret societies as evil. For the Freemasons there was more trouble at the edges when fresh investigations reopened across Europe due to the Inquisition which was a repression of religious heresy from the Catholic Church and set its sights on the Freemasons' society. In 1736 the masonic lodge of Florence, the capital town of Florence, Italy, was examined all the way from bottom to top in 1736, aAuthorities were able to determine that the lodge was founded through an English born Freemason with the name Charles Sackville, the 2nd Duke of Dorset. Sackville was seeking Italians as well as other Englishmen who resided in Italy. Charles Radclyffe, the 5th Earl of Derwentwater was appointed as to be the Grand Master of French Freemasons on the 26th day of December the following year.

Sackville

The situation only changed to the worst. The Scottish-born author Andrew Michael Ramsay, had been chosen to give a speech on the day that Radclyffe was elected. In 1737 Ramsay wrote a revised version of his speech to Cardinal André-Hercule de Fleury, who was also serving as Chief Minister of the King Louis XV of France. In his letter Ramsay had included an application for the official acceptance of the French mason lodges. In lieu of giving Ramsay's blessings, the cardinal who was uninterested in the message was angry and wrote his Freemasons to be branded "traitors" towards and against the Catholic Church. In the following days he banned members of the French Chapter of the Society. These tensions, along with ongoing investigations taking place in Italy and Italy, only grew.

Andre-Hercule de Fleury

The following year on the 28th of April in the year 2000, Pope Clement XII released the first of the papal bans against masonics and referred to them as "In emynti Apostolatus." If the Brotherhoods of the Holy See sign any further ungodly swearing, they'd be punished with "grave penalty." Pope Clement XII also stated that "to be a part of these associations wasexactly the same as acquiring the tarnish of infamy and evil." In the event that Freemasons were in fact not associated with any crime or committing any crime, they would not have such a desire to hide their actions from the general public. The pope concludedthat "The secrecy societies known as the Freemasons are corrupt and depraved. They pose a grave threat for the souls of the faith. Therefore...we require that every Catholic will ever attempt to enter or promote these Freemasons with the risk of excommunication."

Pope Clement XII

Many reiterations of the bans were issued in the years following. The group had achieved the sort of fame that they were reported to have been condemned by at eleven popes. All over Europe the phobia and the propagandism against secret societies carried through to the last decade this century. As for Britain Parliament was also becoming more doubtful about the growing matrix of secret societies within their vicinity. This was especially evident towards the end of the 1790s when the threat of an French invasion continuously looming above.

In 1799's spring, Henry Thornton, a Parliamentary from Southwark the district of Central London, still freshly shocked by a particular report wrote a letter. The letter, which was confidential, was sent towards William Wickham, the Undersecretary of the Home Office, a department which dealt with immigration, counter-terrorism, as well as other related issues. Thornton said that a liquor producer known by the name of

"Benwell," had approached him to seek advice on an employee who had been asked to join an unofficial club located in Wandsworth. He was skeptical and refused the invitation, as the club membership could only be confirmed by the signing of a threatening vow. It also appeared too promising to be true, since he was supposed to get an seven-shilling (roughly $37.50 USD at present) to be present at a meeting, as well as two shillings plus the equivalent of 6 cents ($93.50 USD) for each new member that he drew in. Wickham was enthralled by the scheme of pay-for-stay was compelled by Benwell to convince his employee to sign a petition to join the organization, so they could collect information to strengthen the case against these unsavory organisations.

These stories were not uncommon in the past, and just exacerbated the fear of secret societies. In 1799, the Parliament passed the "Unlawful Society Act of 1799" that banned any secret society that required its members swear vows. While the act was adopted with primarily members of the Jacobites as well as various other Catholic fraternities the Freemasons too felt the heat. It was only after a lengthy debate, and bolstered by collaboration of lodges from different lodges against House of Commons, that the act was changed to exclude Freemasons. There is a belief that a significant majority of monarchists as well as Parliament members were members of grand and masonic lodges which helped to tilt the rule to their advantage.

Even even with the exemption, Freemasons were now required to adhere to a new set of rules. The addresses and names of all visitors and members attending masonic events were to be kept by the Junior Warden and then submitted by the Clerk of Peace, on an annual basis. This law would be in force for a long time until it was removed by the Parliament in the year 1967.

While in America, in the United States, the movement was able to gain momentum that was unheard of in the history of masonic initiation. In 1730 in 1730, The Grand Lodge of England issued warrants to approve the creation of Provincial Grand Lodges in the colonies in North America. Provincial Grand Lodges of Pennsylvania Provincial Grand Lodge of Pennsylvania is believed to have been established in 1731 is said that it is the oldest lodge of masonics within the United States, a claim which is disputed by Grand Lodges of Massachusetts and Virginia that were established within a short time. Between 1733 and 1737 between 1733 and 1737, the Grand Lodge of England issued more warrants , which allowed Freemason flags to be installed within New York and South Carolina.

Many of the founders and famous heroes in America United States were said to be Freemasons. The most famous of the Freemasons was none less than Benjamin Franklin. The Bostonian genius born in 1706 was soon a target for people around him, captivated by his extraordinary ability and potential. Franklin was a prolific writer, inventor philosopher, politician and was a true jack-of-all trades, but hewas also was a revered fellow crafter.

Franklin

When exactly Franklin was admitted to his membership in the Freemasons is still a matter of debate, however many believe that it was in the time of 1731, when Franklin joined the St. John's Lodge of Philadelphia.

The following year, Franklin was 26 years old. Franklin was elevated to the rank of Junior Grand Warden for the Provincial Grand Lodge in Pennsylvania and was promoted into Grand Master status in 1734. In the same year the Grand Master Franklin issued a revised version of the Anderson's 1723 Constitutions which became the first publication of masonics in the United States. It was in 1752 that Franklin was the chairman of a group which was tasked with constructing the first physical foundation of Freemasons in the United States.

Franklin was also praised for his diplomacy skills that proved useful when he was commissioned to help fellow colonists in overseas. He was an ambassador for his lodge, the Philadelphia lodge, and was meticulously participating in numerous meetings across Europe and was appointed The Grand Provincial Master of an annual conference of members of the Grand Lodge of England in November 1760. At the end of 1778 Franklin received a visit to Paris for a meeting where he was to make a deal for French admission in the American Revolution. In his time in Paris Franklin was also charged with coordinating the support of one of the greatest Enlightenment legends, Voltaire, in his candidature for a seat in the Lodge of Nine Sisters. Franklin maintained his affiliation to The Nine Sisters.

It wouldn't be long before the Freemasons of America were caught up in reports that were proclaimed by the general public. It was difficult for many to overlook the fact that the Freemasons were a part of a philosophy that was remarkably similar to the nation's ideals of democracy and the restructuring of social relations. In the end, many began to believe of the Freemasons were puppeteers of their time, the American Revolution.

In the beginning Many of the leading figures of the Revolution which included Benjamin Franklin, George Washington, Samuel Adams, and Alexander Hamilton, were said to be Freemasons at some period of the past. Due to the supposed influence of these figures The number of Freemasons across the country saw an exponential rise. By 1779, there was around 21 , lodges within Massachusetts alone. Within the next two decades, that number almost doubled.

In this light Modern historians have been quick to find holes in these assertions. First, there is no evidence to support the claim there was any evidence that Thomas Jefferson, John Adams, James Madison, Richard Henry Lee or Hamilton - - all of whose names were mentioned - were Freemasons. The historians claim that those who spread these stories believed they were "grossly inflating" the role played by the Freemasons during the Revolution. In addition Of the 56 people that signed the Declaration of Independence, only 9 or 8 were confirmed as Freemasons. This is a number that has been wildly altered over time.

A century later, another intriguing theory was presented by the author Joseph Fort Newton. Newton believed that it was been Freemasons who planned the Boston Tea Party. According to his theories, most of those who fought on boats came members of an Freemason group known under the descriptor of the "Caucus Pro Bono Publico" and are believed to have conducted their planning in the Green Dragon Tavern. On the 16th of December 1773, the Freemason rebels, with Samuel Adams and the Sons of Liberty and others dressed to appear as Mohawk Indians, stole away in the dark. They entered an Boston vessel, grabbed the vessel and threw 342 tea chests across the decks. Some of the rebels who were aboard was Paul Revere, who later became the Grand Master of the Provincial Lodge in Massachusetts, and Thomas Crafts, John Hancock along with Joseph Warren, all confirmed Freemasons.

Revere

Hancock

Despite the bustling rumor mills, the amount of Freemasons in America was still experiencing an increase of about 10. In the 18th century the nation experienced an explosion of lodges with independent status. Green lodges realized that necessary paperwork to authorize them would be expensive and time-consuming in the absence of a grand lodge was in the land of the mother. In spite of this, the lodges went ahead by themselves and only sought approval when they were sure their community would last at least 10 years.

The 13th of October 1792 was another significant day in the history of Freemasonry. The day that marked the event, George

Washington, the first President of the United States, aided by Joseph Clark, the Grand Master of a lodge located in Maryland and gathered to lay the foundation stone for the United States Capitol in a ritual of masonic ceremonies. Three Worshipful Masters also attended, with offerings of corn, oil, and wine in the spirit of Solomon. Solomon. Near the end of the ceremony Washington picked up heaps of dirt using a masonic trowel and the diamond-shaped symbol was buried in the earth. Washington's apron and sash may still be seen inside the Masonic Grand Lodge of Pennsylvania. The trowel was later employed in the cornerstone ceremonies of other historical buildings which include those of the Washington Monument and the Herbert Hoover Building.

Chapter 5: A Print From 1870 Of Washington

As Master Of His Lodge. Lodge

At the beginning of the nineteenth century there was approximately 16000 Freemasons across America. In 1822, the number had risen to 80.000. In order to put it in context, it was about 5 percent of all qualified bachelors across the United States.

The Anti-Masons

"What we've done for ourselves is gone with us. What we've done for other people and the world is undying and lives on forever." Albert Pike. Albert Pike

It seemed like The Freemasonry community in America was at its peak However, all the hard work will soon begin to disintegrate.

William Morgan was born in 1774 in the picturesque city of Culpeper, Virginia. He strayed between the lines of poverty and the lower middle class for his entire existence, starting as a plebeian stone mason and bricklayer, later start his own company in Richmond. In all his years Morgan's credibility has been constantly questioned by his colleagues. Morgan was once boasting to his friends and family that he was an officer in the War of 1812. Although many around him felicitated him for his contribution but historians of the present are uncertain. A few soldiers with his name "William Morgan" were indeed listed on the roster, however they had not come close to holding the position of captain. There is still some doubt as to whether Morgan actually served in the war in any way.

The year 1819 was when a 45 year old Morgan was enthralled by an exquisite 16-year-old girl known as Lucinda Pendleton. They tied the knot in the same year. Two years later, the newlyweds packed up all their belongings and moved north to Canada where they settled. In Canada, Morgan managed his own brewery until a blaze was sparked, devouring everything within the path of.

Morgan

Cracked, Morgan made the slow journey back in the United States. He landed with his family in New York, first camping out in Rochester before settling in Batavia. The dejected Morgan fell down to the depths of his barrel time, and was then forced back to work as a mason who earned a meager salary. Disappointed and frustrated, Morgan resorted to binge drinking and gambling recklessly however, things were going to get very ugly.

In Canada, Morgan had incessantly boasted of his status as Master Mason , to anybody who tried to be amused. Morgan's inconsistent stories blurred the lines between the real and the fiction. While there are reports of Morgan's trips in Freemason Chapters in Virginia however, the question of whether Morgan was actually initiated isn't known.

The fact that has been proven is that Morgan was then refused entry into his Batavia chapter. The people in the Batavia lodge mentioned the general disdain for Morgan's personality as the reason behind the low-profile rejection however, others expressed reservations about his origins. Even with his past of ambiguity, Morgan was accepted into the lodge that was located near Le Roy's Western Star Chapter #33, which was where he received the Royal Arch award. It is not surprising that whether or not Morgan was actually able to complete the previous 6 degrees is open to discussion.

The year was 1826. Morgan was attempting to put the foundation of a masonic chapter at Batavia but was disqualified from this privilege. As a result, the furious Morgan went on the streets to announce the imminent publication of his upcoming publication, Illustrations of Masonry, an all-encompassing book which promised to reveal the dark details of the shady rituals and the esoteric secrets of the organization. To make things more sweet, Morgan claimed that David Miller the publisher of an area newspaper and a friend of his, had offered him an appealing advance prior to the publication.

Within a couple of days of the announcement made, Morgan was arrested and put in prison due to a default on a loan which was a mere L2.60 (approximately 459 dollars in the present). For months after, Morgan's Freemasons were believed that they went to any possible length to make him reconsider his decision. They attempted numerous times to convince him and even went so that they were allegedly burning one of the printing presses in town but to no avail.

The fateful day came around. In the early late hours of the night the assailants made their way into the prison with a scream of sneakiness. A sleepy Morgan was awakened as his attackers dragged him from the cell and put him into a car. As the horse raced across the streets and was disappeared witnesses claimed to hear Morgan's cries breaking the silence "Murder Murder!" Some say that Morgan was simply sent to Canada and others thought the most likely scenario. Whatever the reason, Morgan was never seen again.

A representation of Morgan's assassination

The disturbing events continued. Witnesses disappeared quickly and suffering the same fate. There was no one to talk. Then, a group of local Freemasons were arrested and accused of Morgan's kidnapping as well as murder. The name of DeWitt Hillary Clinton, a former American senator and sixth governor in New York, had surfaced amid the murky stew of accusations. As time passed, the judge, who could not find no credible evidence to identify the perpetrators of the crime, was left with no other option other than to let them go.

Clinton

The general public, particularly New York and surrounding states became angry with the Freemasons and the residents launched an escalating series of violent protests against the organization. The fury led to massive expulsions, which saw members leave in a mass. Half of the lodges were closed in Maryland. The situation was not much better with regard to New York. In 1827, there were 227 lodges registered under the authority under the jurisdiction of Grand Lodge of New York. Over the course of eight years, the number fell to 41.

Thurlow Weed, who was a staunch opponent of Andrew Jackson and the Freemasons He founded The Anti-Masonic Party soon after. The group gained the approval of many prominent politicians among them William H. Seward, and the president John Adams himself. John Adams, the president of America was hostile against Freemasonry that he was so opposed to Freemasons that he later wrote the book Letters on the Masonic Institution, in which the president boldly declared, "I do conscientiously and strongly consider that Freemasonry...is among the biggest ethical and political crimes that the Union is currently working ..."

Weed

In 1832 in 1832, in 1832, the Anti-Masonic Party played a controversial choice in selecting William Hirt, a suspected Freemason who had stood up for the fraternity in numerous instances and was their party's presidential candidate. At Election Day, the party got just 7 electoral votes. By 1835, the Antimasonic party was disbanded in every other state except for Pennsylvania.

The late 1850s saw the Freemason movement was once more leading the group. As they were fighting in the American Civil War started in the early 1890s, the number of Freemasons from America was soaring by 66,000 to 200 000 in the 5,000 lodges spread all over the country. In the course of war, tales of the fraternity's love for one another started to circulate. They were courageous Freemason soldiers were believed to have taken care of wounded warriors and POWs of opposing troops that belonged in the same fraternity.

Just after that the Civil War drew to an end and the Freemasons along as other Brotherhoods entered into the "Golden age of fraternalism." It was the time when this fraternity was brought about thanks to Albert Pike, a mountain of a man, weighing 300 pounds, standing more than 6 feet tall. He was a tall man with an incredibly long and beautiful beard that was as clear as snow. Pike encouraged the fraternity to restore their damaged image in the public spotlight by shifting their attention on charity. It worked. It was in 1872 that Pike wrote Morals and Dogma and the book included a retelling of Freemason history and also the mysterious knowledge that was hidden within the organization. New initiations of 33, including instructions, were introduced in the book, based on a mix of astronomy, old religions, and the traditional mythology of the masonic order. Pike was eventually an icon around which future conspiracy theories and disputes were revolved, with some claiming that his work contains aspects of prejudice and racism.

Pike

Schisms, Schemes, and Modern Freemasons

"Be certain that the wisest words you speak are the ones you don't say." Robert W. Service Robert W. Service

The Freemasonry movement eventually spread throughout the world However, its influence on France was to remain one of the greatest achievements. In the early 1900s, there was about 10.000 Freemasons within France. At the close this century this number was doubled and by the year 1936, that number had increased to an astounding 60,000.

The society initially appealed to men who were attracted to the spiritual aspect of the Freemasons. A lot of members enjoyed socializing with their fellow Freemasons in extravagant outfits and found these elaborate rituals to be thrilling. In the years following when the Freemason tradition developed in France The society grew into an important hub for French business and politics.

Gradually gradually, the French Freemasons began to drift away from their main ideology of equality in society and ethics-based living. A growing number of politicians joined the organization along with other civil servants, with the intention of gaining an even bigger platform and a greater chance of getting elected or promoted. Hotel managers and innkeepers are also a big part of the pie looking to expand their client base. Businessmen also took advantage of the chance to meet with colleagues and identify the possibility of new opportunities for business. Another benefit was the discount of 10% every Freemason got on every transaction or purchase with a brother.

In a moment of déjà of a previous episode in which the French public started to become skeptical of the Freemasons. If they couldn't find answers, they decided to create their own. They claimed that the Freemasons of controlling the government behind the scenes , and of propagating propaganda that promoted the anti-religion movement and other views that were materialist.

In any case the modern historians claim that these claims are exaggerated. Although the French Freemasons were indeed in favor of some anti-religious beliefs but these views have existed prior to their arrival. The tensions between the Freemasons were exacerbated at the beginning of the 20th century.

A radical group led by the War Minister Emile Combes reached an arrangement in 1904 with the Grand Orient de France Lodge. As part of the agreement they agreed that the Freemasons were charged with monitoring a variety of army officers, focusing on their political and religious opinions. The spies then set about whipping an smear campaign to discredit the Catholics. This plan was ultimately stopped which led to the removal from Combes in 1905 and ultimately the dissolution of the group. The scandalous incident is now referred to in the form of the "Affaire Des Fiches."

Combes

As time passed it was discovered that the French Freemasons discovered a new enemy within The English chapter. The seeds of distrust were believed to have been planted at an gathering in the Grand Orient de France in 1877. It was determined by a vote that it was the right time to amend the constitution that was in vogue. The constitution was originally written as "Its principals include

God's existence, the immortality of God and the immortality of souls as well as human unity." It is now said, "Its principles are absolute freedom of conscience as well as humanity's cooperation." In the end, United Grand Lodge of England was stunned by the revelation. They promptly issued a response with a firm statement that they would not be able to with good conscience, acknowledge brothers who deny the existence of God "Great Creator of the Universe," namely, God or any other supreme being.

The tense tensions only got worse after that. The French were not happy with the English chapter's association with Crown and Protestant Church. At the opposite end of the spectrum The English were furious at the French brothers' desire to degrade one of social's most fundamental beliefs that was a firm belief of the Almighty. In spite of the English chapter's fervent opinion on the matter and their ties to their counterparts in the Grand Orient of Belgium, who also opted to include the notion of an ultimate being in their constitution, was not affected. Naturally, this has affected the relationship between the fraternities.

None of these rumors can be as convincing as those that came out around the time of the 1800s. In 1885 the French writer Marie Joseph Jogand-Pages (pen title Leo Taxil), converted to the Catholic faith. This was particularly shocking because for many years his controversial anti-Catholic beliefs were the bread and butter of his life. In the absence of a needed break, Taxil's itchy fingers quickly discovered a new pen. He was facing a new foe in his mind: the Freemasons. Through the 1890s, Taxil churned out volumes of pamphlets and other books in which he revealed the vile and secret practices of the fraternity. The claims became more absurd with every publication, which focused on allegations of the group's apparent dedication to Satan as well as other bizarre like cult-like behavior, complete with eyewitness accounts. One of Taxil's works, Devil in the Nineteenth Century is believed to be composed by an author called Diane Vaughan who purportedly took part in rituals of Satan. Her numerous encounters with demons from the underworld evoked the psychedelic effects of drugs, which included an incident of a demon being tipped by on the piano's keys. crocodile shaped piano.

Taxil

Taxil's novels became instant bestsellers, and gathered an almost entirely Catholic following. When Vaughan continued to publish several more books and her followers requested an appearance on the public stage. In April 1897, Taxil determined to give public what they desired and organized an event for press conferences. The crowd waited with eager breath and waited for Taxil to declare that it was he alone who wrote the books. And, perhaps more shockingly was the fact that he shrewdly declared that nothing that he wrote on the Freemasons was authentic, and then he went on to express his gratitude to the Catholic newspaper for allowing him to tell his bizarre stories. In the end, he acknowledged that Vaughan was nothing less than a secretary who was more than willing to let him utilize her name in the long-running scam.

The Freemasons remain an extremely popular topic for conspiracy theorists in the present. In addition to the usual speculations about alleged warmongers bent to rule the world or reptiles wearing human skin suits, the Freemasons have been the subject of many theories, ranging from the absurd and humorous to the shocking.

One of the most humorous stories centers around one of the most humorous stories revolves around Latrobe Brewing Company, based in Pennsylvania. The label on one of their most popular beers "Rolling Rock" has an inscription that reads "33" near the conclusion of one the passages. A lot of people jumped the gun one time and believed it was a reference to the "33" was in reference to the 33rd degree of Scotland's Rite. The story was dispelled in 1986, when a journalist realized that the "33" was simply a reference to the number of words within the sentence. It was just mistaken.

Theorists of conspiracy claim to have discovered some surprising information about the location in Washington D.C.. The Masonic square and compass are believed to be seen from an aerial perspective. The capital is located on highest point of the compass. The capital is connected by one axis with the White House, and the other connects it to the Jefferson Memorial. Then there is the Lincoln Memorial. Lincoln Memorial is connected with both White House and Jefferson

Memorial creating the square and completes the image. Although this concept may sound however, it has been debunked by many historians. According to the bubble-bursters these patterns and connections are a given for cities that are built in grids but they are not exclusive.

Some of these conspiracy theories inspired by Freemason are presented with a sinister twist. One of these theories claims it is that Albert Pike, whose works have been accused of being white supremacist propaganda, created the famous Ku Klux Klan. Although theories like this have been proven false repeatedly however, they can be seen on numerous websites.

A conspiracy theorist named Billy Morgan, takes his theories to the next level. He claims to be the one to uncover the most secretive and most sinister of Freemason secrets: ritual sodomy. The practice, Morgan insists, is an attempt to control the mind that is mostly used on children aged between 2 to 4. The procedure is believed to cause memory blackouts, as well as a mental journey that can open the "third eyes to Luciferian light." As for the absurdity Modern historians agree these claims are utterly fake and defamatory. They were created by the fantasies of incredibly imaginative minds.

Today Freemasons, and the numerous affiliate organizations all over the world continue to make progress, giving hundreds of millions of dollars to charities each year. The Freemasons have lodges on every continent in the globe, except for Antarctica. In 2016 they reported that the United Grand Lodge of England recorded one quarter of one million Freemasons under its jurisdiction and 6 million in the world and approximately 2 million members located in the United States.

It's certain that regardless of what people consider Freemasons, their legacy will last for a long time.

Chapter 6: The Peasants' Revolt

After Edward II came Edward III. The previous king's reign was thought to be an unfortunate one. Unending disputes between a number of barons of high rank and other noblemen were a major issue during his reign as King. Particularly his relationship with a man called Piers Gaveston caused a stir across the kingdom. It is unclear exactly the circumstances that led to this controversy however, it was enough to trigger legal chaos and an ongoing struggle to gain the power. At the end of the day, Gaveston was caught and executed by the barons. The result was a prolonged period of war, which included barons based in Scotland. Edward II fought them and sought to end the conflict in his own realm and an ongoing disagreement over Scotland itself. In addition, Gaveston had also managed to cause a stir in France and his relations with the King was causing problems on two fronts. The barons' battle with Edward resulted in the English King being defeated by an unnamed Scot called Robert the Bruce in 1314. The loss left an indelible impression, and the repercussions were felt through conflict and famine in the majority of England. Critiques of the King were abound.

Edward II seemed unable to satisfy his opponents. After a protracted disagreement-- involving betrayals, legislation, and executions--with the Scottish, he was forced into signing a peace treaty with Robert the Bruce. The same issue was arising in his dealings with France after 1325, when Edward sent the wife of his Isabella in France to discuss a peace treaty. It was believed that Isabella was the ideal candidate. Because she was the princess of the French King, and a bride who Edward had specifically married to create peace. When she was brought to France but she was unable to return and refused to even negotiate an agreement with her home country. Instead she found an ally and launched an attack on her new homeland. In 1326 with an army in her back, Isabella and her alliance were able to wage war against Edward II. The King, afraid of his own life and caught between the belligerents of the south and north and west, ran to west. He sought shelter in Wales however he was captured just a few months after. The king was forced forfeit the crown, which led to his controversial rule ending in January 1327. He passed the crown to Edward III, his fourteen year old son. A mere year later, the former king passed away under unidentified circumstances, possibly murdered at the direction from the new government.

Despite his age the reign of Edward III was far more prosperous. Although he was crowned in 1327 but he was ruled until 1377. For the next fifty more years Edward III fought to make England as a significant actor in European political life. Although the previous ruler had diminished the influence of the country and influence, the new king boosted the military power of the country. He fought for a long time and with great determination against France and the French, launching the known as the Hundred Years War and seeing huge victories for his country. However, at home it wasn't as impressive. The outbreak of Black Death, a plague which struck the entire country and killed thousands as well as entire villages and towns were suddenly devastated. In his final years his health also began to decline. In the 14th century his ability to rule was hindered by his ill health which, by 1377 the king died of stroke. The crown was handed over to Richard II Richard II, the king's ten-year old grandson, whose father had passed away in the previous year.

Then why do we have to go through all this in a book on the Freemasons? The turmoil that swept through England during the 14th Century is a way to divert our attention from the awe in the dissolution of Knights Templar. At the time Richard II ascended the throne and was crowned, it appeared that the Templars were long gone. With a new King on the throne with England becoming a major power in the political arena, along with France and Scotland being squelched up to not any longer being a serious threat and it appeared England could be set to enjoy a lengthy period of prosperity. However, it wasn't to be.

In the time before the Reformation that was pre-Reformation, in the pre-Reformation era, Catholic Church was among the sole true international organizations. It had some influence in nearly every single community in Europe. This was especially true in England as well. The Church wasn't free of the greed and corruption which caused the anger of the peasants. The inherent conflict between being an agent of good and being prone to corruption, reflected an identical contradiction, one that could have been a concern for members of the deported Knights Templar. The Templars were initially an Catholic militant group which was a reflection of the church's military power. They were later disqualified and imprisoned by the same organization they had pledged to defend. According to certain scholars, it was the decision of the Vatican that ended the loyalty between church members and Templars. After their exile, the Templars became a group without a leader. They could choose whatever side they chose.

The Church was divided. It was in 1377 that the temporary residence for the Pope in Avignon was closed. In 1377, Pope Gregory XI returned the home of the Church to Rome and was astonished of Cardinals. After moving to France and becoming closer to the French monarchy that had banned those known as the Knights Templar, the Catholic Church was gaining an French flavour. The return to Italy was unpopular with the French population. After Gregory passed away and an election of a new pope took place and riots broke out on Rome's streets Rome affected the decision to have the first Italian on the top spot in

Christendom. Despite the fact that the pope Urban VI promised to keep the foundations of the church within the Vatican however, the French priests were not happy. The result was the most significant schism in church history. The Great Schism, the church was divided into two distinct groups in 1378. In addition to the Pope's Pope Urban VI in Rome The French Cardinals chose the country's own Pope, Clement VII, to be the head of the church from Avignon. Alongside the support of cardinals from all over the world the countries started to declare their support. Through Clement VII, came France, Scotland, Portugal, Spain, and various German principalities. In Urban VI came England, Poland, Hungary and the majority of the Holy Roman Empire and others who were considered to be enemies of France which was perhaps the most powerful state in Europe in the time. Each camp excommunicated the priests from the other and declared itself to be the only true church.

Then France as well as England were engaged in a traditional war. They were also taking opposing sides in a spiritual war. They required funds and they needed to get them fast. In England this was the tax on polls of 1377.

The 1381 introduction poll taxes caused an uproar. The peasants were angry. The peasants were at war with powerful landowners for a long time, and their position changed due to the effects caused by the Black Death. The power of barons was increased under previous monarchs, but the devastation of the Black Death had drastically reduced the number of people working. A three-quarters of people passed away. The subsequent famines cost more. The peasants were increased in demand, and their bargaining power improved. Although the peasants wanted to benefit from this bleak situation, the increase in their wages occurred at the cost of the landowners who were the owners of the land. Because landowners now having a larger number of powers, they arranged to pass laws that restricted the amount they paid peasants. The wages were reduced to levels that they were prior to the outbreak. Additionally, the details of the peasant's lineage were recorded and efforts were to tie people permanently to a specific Lord. The concept of serfdom was also incorporated into law. The tensions started to rise.

The underlying grievances of the family came to an end in the spring of 1381, when a rebellion was sparked within Kent as well as Essex. The ensuing conflict would being known as the Peasants Revolt. The group was led by Wat Tyler and other leaders The peasants started to form large groups. They protested, going as that they set fire to Savoy Palace and kill members of the King's court. They demanded the dismantling of serfdom, the feudal system of government which left the working poor ruled by the wishes of the person who owned the land they resided. His court and the King would flee back to Tower of London and quickly realize that they didn't have the power to take on the thousands of peasants. They'd need to negotiate.

The position of the King was not secure. He was only fourteen and dependent on the counsel of his inner circle and his inner circle, but the kingdom wasn't as financially secure as he would have liked. The conflicts of his grandfather, and his success in the establishment of England as a powerhouse in the military was expensive. Funds had been drained. And to make matters worse the rise of an untried king appeared to encourage corruption in the court. To counter this the crown had enacted various more invasive and perverse taxes which were again imposed on the poor. One of them was the poll tax that was one of the primary causes for the revolt. As much as the landowners and barons the king's financial insufficiency were the primary blame. In desperate need of money, and facing conflict from all sides, England had erupted into revolt. To make matters more complicated it appeared that there was some sort of plotting behind the event.

It's been said it was the case that the Peasants' Rebellion was not spontaneous. The numerous whispers of revolt and rebellion were sparked across the nation as the various lines of conflict facing the authorities started to unite at once. People like John Ball, the leader of a group of priests who stood with the poor and those who were in need who were in need, ignited the flames of rebellion across the country. The various communities across the country were urged to take action to protest, up to 100,000 peasants came together to express their displeasure with the monarchy.

The first indications of a revolt were when tax collectors were beat to death while they carried out their job. The local lord was attempting to forcefully collect his tax and tried to get the crowd of people who were defying the law and beaten up, police officers were slapped while the local lord got fortunate to flee to London. After the government reacted with a much larger army to stop the riot the crowd reacted with renewed determination. Prosecutors weren't just nabbed and executed, but also beheaded. In the beginning, in Essex similar incidents occurred in Kent as well as the regions around London. The mob started to increase in size and people flocked from towns and villages across the country to demonstrate against the king.

In the crowd of thousands, a single man was seen to emerge as leader. In the absence of any provocation people soon began to look towards a man called Walter (or Wat) Tyler to receive instructions. The rebellion even adopted its name with lots of people calling the revolt Wat Tyler's Revolt. There isn't much about the man, or the place he was from or what his primary complaint was. Why did millions of people all of a sudden agreed to the man as their leader? It's hard to know however, many have believed this as a sign that there is a higher level of general understanding than is apparent in our day and day and.

While Wat Tyler and the rest of his team walked through Canterbury in the midst of beheading "traitors" as they went the same civic turmoil in Essex was followed. On the same day Tyler as well as his men attended an enormous mass at Canterbury Cathedral, the men of Essex were burning down a significant building that belonged to the Knights Hospitallers. The structure was important. It was originally owned by the Knights Templar and was given by them to the Knights Templar in 1138 through the royal decree. In the period when the Templars were sacked and evicted away from Christendom and retreated from the world, it fell into the hands of the Hospitallers. In fact they Hospitallers were among the principal beneficiaries of the decision to pursue the Templars and took on a large portion of their assets and holdings as well as a substantial portion of their assets. In the following days there would be a number in the Hospitallers most valuable structures and homes were targeted by rebels, presumably in the context of larger social turmoil, but much more than any other group. Could it be an accident that the leadership of rebels was so determined to confront the enemy that was the Knights Templar? This is where we begin to understand the interconnection of the threads and narratives moving in place from the Crusades hundreds of years before.

On the 11th day of June the two rebel groups chose to change their tactics and marched towards the capital. In the end the total number of rebels was over 100,000. Even though they were separated and untrained historians were amazed by the determination and discipline shown by the protesters. It was a seventy-mile trip that took two days and both groups arrived mostly around the same time. It's easy to understand why so many have suggested that this event was planned, not just a random event.

At this point that the teen king fled to his Tower of London. He accompanied him with the most reliable advisors he had, the people he could count on to help him in making decisions. Included among them were archbishops of Canterbury and the treasurer of the king who was part of the Hospitallers. Additionally, there was one known as Henry

Bolingbroke, who would later be a household name for his role as the future King England. There were also barons, earls and other members of the aristocracy each of them were frightened by the peasants, who had become a scourge.

In June 12th The rebels were forming a mass in the area that is now East London. They moved across the river, and then moved through Southwark. From across London increasing numbers of people joined them. As groups of rebels formed in various parts of the city and decided to burn and sack palaces, paying particular attention paid to the documents kept by the aristocracy. They kept records of lineage and genealogy that were used to tie people to serfdom. Prisons were attacked, and the prisoners were thrown out.

From in the Tower of London, the young King could observe the smoke rising out of his capital city. To counter he sent out messages to the rebels asking them what they desired. The reply he received told him that the rebels were seeking in reality to rescue the King. They wanted to remove him from the gang of traitors who had surrounded him and committed their lives to devastation of the country. The king demanded an assembly, asking rebels to stop their devastation of the city, so that the king could hear their complaints fully.

The rebels were in agreement. They were moved towards the river, with and the Kent men were on their way, Kent located on the southern side , and those who came from Essex located on the North side. The king departed on his way to his home at the Tower of London on his royal barge. He slowed his speed as he sailed through the river, aiming to make contact with rebels. In the middle of his voyage that his advisers were able to convince the king to slow down. When it became clear that the king had stopped their march, the rebels made direct demands to the barge. In the first place the barge had a list of people who were to be executed. A large portion of those who were listed were aboard the Royal Barge that moment, which included the prior to the Hospitallers and the Archbishop of Canterbury. It is not surprising that the council of the King's Council strongly opposed such a move. From the shore the rebels could watch the barge of the King turn and return to the Tower.

The rebels went into the city in the proper area. In a strange twist of luck, neither gate they went to was found to be secured. Unhindered, they marched straight through. Abstaining from sacking and degrading all that was in their way Instead, they marched directly towards Fleet Street, an important area of London which also housed an inmate. They attacked, releasing all prisoners.

In close proximity were two forges that had been once the property of the Knights Templar. They were being managed under the control of Hospitallers. As before, the rebels poured their ire at forges. They destroyed each them. When they made their way through the city to Savoy Palace Savoy Palace, the mob was only able to target every building they could verify for belonging to the Hospitallers. They destroyed a number of buildings, however, none of them were subject to the fury of the mob as much than that of the Savoy Palace. Furniture, art work tapestries, furniture, and other important items had been destroyed to the point of no repair. Once they had finished they began to burn the palace and assisted in the cause by making sure a quantity of gunpowder kegs was first brought into the.

When Savoy Palace was destroyed, the rebels began to pay attention to any buildings controlled and managed under Knights Hospitaller. Knights Hospitaller. Anything that could be located between Thames as well as Fleet Street was vandalized and later burnt. Records were burnt and lawyers who be able to resist the crowd were shot dead. The only Hospitaller property that seemed to be safe from damage was a tiny church. But, the rebels entered the church and took all the records they could. These were then burned on the street. It's possible that the church had was formerly owned by The Knights Templar. It was among the few buildings that were not totally destroyed. When you compare it with it's counterpart, the Hospitaller Headquarters in Clerkenwell which was destroyed beyond repair It is an unbeliever that the Templars old church could be able to escape with such ease.

The rebels continued their fight. They marched through the city, freeing prisoners and burning documents with particular attention paid at Hospitaller properties. One group, having tried to ask for an audience with the Tower of London for an audience with the King was refused. They then laid an attack on the Tower. The fact that it was possibly the most secure structure in England was not a factor that seemed to be a matter of concern for them.

In the entire area, the city revealed that being an official or the Exchequer or Chancery (two authorities that are part of our nation's tax collection authorities) could condemn an individual to death. In the case of proving crimes, the appearance of ink on someone's fingers was enough to prove his guilt. Since the majority of educated men received their education through the church, it's not a coincidence that the majority of the deceased were clergymen.

The king appeared stunned. At this point, he has no reaction to the rebellion. Without an army to fight the massive crowd of rebels and the funds to pay for the crowds and the time necessary to tackle an organized revolt The King was in a dilemma in deciding how to respond. Instead of a display of strength or force it was necessary to use tricks to win over his adversaries. On June 14 the news was released that the king was willing to meet with rebels, in the hope of accepting all their demands. The message was sent to the town criers throughout the city, and then broadcast for everyone to be able to hear.

As a venue for meetings The King and his advisors picked Mile End, a place with fields that just was outside the city's walls. The goal was to drive the rebels away from the city in the first place. The goal was achieved with a significant portion of the troops going after the king beyond the city's walls. However, not all did so. Wat Tyler, and couple hundred others remained throughout the capital city with a plot to come up with their own.

Even in the morning of the scheduled meeting there was a hiccup in the camp of the king. When they set out to confront the rebels archbishops from Canterbury was caught trying to get a boat to get away down the Thames. The riverbanks were populated with people who were aware of him, and the protest and admonition from the river's banks compelled the oarsmen to resign and return back to their Tower.

The king set out for the conference, taking his trusted advisers. The records are careful to mention the individuals who traveled with the king, they do not provide information about the individuals who were not. Particularly Sir Simon Sudbury and Sir Robert Hales aren't listed. In other words that Sir Robert Hales is the archbishop of Canterbury and the prelate of the Knights Hospitaller. If they stayed at the Tower or were required to stay there isn't evident. There is no details of who was given the leadership role within the rebel camp on that day while the most infamous leaders, such those of Wat Tyler or John Ball remained in the city, despite having a hidden purpose.

It appeared that the meeting in Mile End would go well. The meeting was accompanied by two requests made by the rebels. They demanded that they be allowed to pursue and kill anyone they believed as a traitor to the king as well as the populace. The second was that the serfdom system be abolished, and every Englishman being a free man. The response of the king seemed to be reasonable. In response to the first request, the king agreed that "terrorists" were to be punished in the event that they were found to be guilty by an audiencia or court of law. In response to the second request the clerks gathered in the thirty clerks that had gathered along with him, specially designed to create legislation in a short measure.

The meeting between rebels and the King appeared to be working however, the events in the city continued to unfold. The rebels hit. Wat Tyler and the gang intended to attack and take the Tower of London itself. A lofty goal even in the most tense of times not to mention with just 100 or so lightly armoured rebels. The Tower was already the most fortified structure in the nation The Tower was protected by hundreds of soldiers who were professional. The Tower had a drawbridge portcullis and a gate that was heavy and the vast arsenal of weapons used by the soldiers inside. In addition, the troops inside the Tower were given Robert Hales, prior of the Knights Hospitaller and a proven battle commander, who was able to teach the troops.

However, Tyler and his men took on the rebels. It appeared that the rebels had a person inside. When the rebels arrived they found that the drawbridge was gone. The portcullis was lifted. The gate was now open.

The rebels entered London's Tower of London and the historians fought to record the rage of their word while they did so.

After gaining entry into the Tower The rebels retreated to take on their enemies. They targeted the archbishop. Canterbury was their first target . They were able to locate them in the church. After dragging him out into the open They beat him, and threw him on the floor. Then another group arrived along with the similarly unarmed Hospitaller. The two men were confined at bay while rebels searched the tower for men they wanted to target; Tax collectors, Lords and so on. After they had found all the men they needed, they brought the two men up to Tower Hill. Amid a cheering public, they cut off the heads of each man. The headless heads were then removed and put on poles on London Bridge for all to observe. To honor the archbishop's former station the archbishop's distinctive mitre and attached the head of the archbishop to it.

After the executions, rebels spread all over the city. They searched for other victims who were on their list, individuals who caused conflict. They found more than 160 dead who they killed. Of the dead, there were those who were incorrupt and the traitorous (as determined by the rebels) as well as any person who voiced their opinions against them or even praised the recently dead.

A special mission was arranged by Tyler. He put together an uninvolved group and dispatched the rebels out of London and towards Highbury and Highbury, with the intention to destroy a particular structure. It was also a part of the Hospitallers and was recently restored by the Order and was deemed to be an extremely extravagant and luxurious houses in the area.

It wasn't long before the word of this assault to be spread to Mile End's King and the people in Mile End. The meeting was canceled and the king fled to his residence at Castle Baynard, clearly not intending to return back to his home in the Tower of London. The team of clerks charged with drafting the legislation were busy with their work. The king had left the scene, and several rebels had taken pages from clerks, returning to their homes to proclaim the royal decree.

The next event is unclear and not recorded in the books of history. The King was willing to meet with the rebels once more but this time at Smithfield. The meeting was scheduled for the following day, that is, the 15th June. Prior to the meeting, the monarch attended the church during the service at Westminster Abbey. He was followed to the altar by a few rebels who were curious about what was going on. While there they came across a disgusting tax collector within one of the churches. Despite his appeal for mercy, the man was taken out in the open and executed in front of crowds. The king was finished with the mass and then left to Smithfield.

A large number of rebels were waiting to see the king. They were gathered along one side, and the King as well as his troops were lining up on the other. What transpired next is a hot debate in the historical books. There is a claim that Wat Tyler was one of the rebel leaders, and his brutal insults hurled at the king caused a lot of skepticism and that his conduct was thought to be a slap towards the crown a certain manner. Most likely, this was likely to give the King as well as his troops the reason they needed for them to carry in the direction of the plan for the entire time. It went in the following manner.

On opposite side of the field the king pleaded for to see the commander of rebels. This was Wat Tyler. In order to make the request, Tyler summoned William Walworth, the mayor of London himself William Walworth, across the field. Tyler realizing that an appearance with the King would be far from his soldiers and outnumbered, became suspicious. He devised hand signals that was, if it was implemented, would mean that rebels must immediately begin attacking. His instructions were that in such an attack each member of the opposing forces must be killed, apart from the King. In the company of just one soldier carrying his banner, Wat Tyler walked out on the field.

It's interesting that we have only official account of what happened afterward. A majority of those are, as it appears, not present. According to their account--the only one we have--it appears like Wat Tyler had a meeting with the King. He then issued his demands again. The demands were a lot higher. The demands had increased. Tyler was requesting the property of the church to be taken away and the money distributed to the less fortunate, he also wanted many legal changes, and demanded that only one bishop be elected for the entire country of England.

While Tyler went through his demands front of the King, William Walworth silently drew his dagger. He slipped behind the leader of the rebellion the mayor cut him in the neck. One of the squires of the King came to aid, pulling out a knife and then stabbing Tyler twice. The rebel was trying to return towards his soldiers, he fell off his horse. The wound was severe. He was not going to live.

On the other side of the field wasn't certain what had transpired. The hand signal which was in place prior to the time Tyler was gone was not visible. Instead, they witnessed an unidentified rider emerge from across the wide expanse, and advancing toward them. It was King George and the 14 year old boy. He addressed the rebels to inform the rebels that he was pleased to satisfy their demands, and to accompany him to Clerkenwell-the location in which the Hospitaller palace is still burning to sign the agreement. Then, he took off out, with his soldiers as well as his army.

The rebels were confused. They weren't sure the best way to act. A group of people walked out onto the field on their own and found Tyler's body. The man was in a state of death, evidently and was transported to the nearby hospital to find out what was possible to do. Over the span of an hour trying to find an approach, the well-organized rebels decided they would adhere to the instructions of the king. They left to Clerkenwell.

Unbeknownst to themwas that anti-rebellion groups were already getting ready to form a mass. Perhaps motivated by the news of Wat Tyler's death, a multitude were congregating. The Mayor, the King and a host of other power leaders issued a call to all men who were physically able to join forces against the rebels.

As they entered Clerkenwell and the rebels immediately demanded that King hand over all those who had been involved the murder of Wat Tyler's killing. When the rebels argued their argument to the king, the anti-rebellion crowd was gathered around. Slowly, with the rebels not being aware of who they are, the anti-rebellion mob were surrounded by rebels. The leader eventually was able inform the King that he was in the superiority. In observing that the rebels were at present surrounded and outnumbered by the king, the king ordered that they disperse or get punished due to their conduct.

Recognizing that the tables had changed the crowd of rebels began to split up. The next time, there was no order. They fled in dribs and dabs, the only group that was truly organized that was controlled by John Ball, the preacher who led a band of rebels to the city across London Bridge. After having passed triumphantly just three days earlier the incident, they now fled the city.

The Mayor William Walworth went looking for the leader of the rebellion, Wat Tyler. He discovered Tyler at the hospital close to Smithfield and his wounds were being treated by nurses. Although the wounds were probably fatal Walworth decided not to risk it. He pulled Tyler from his hospital bed and into the streets. Like many rebels' victims Tyler was struck in the head off. The head was replaced those heads that were slain by the King's men on the poles over London Bridge.

A large portion of the king's inner circle were knighted. They helped in the fight to keep an insurgent from the town. But they were not completely addressed the problem. Outside of London the city, a large number of people were angry. The anger over the tax system and the treatment of the poor wasn't only restricted only to Essex as well as Kent. In fact, during the time prior to and following the Peasants' Revolution There were protests all across the nation.

The reports from Suffolk revealed that a local pastor had brought together angry locals to set fire to the home that belonged to a corrupt nobleman and then evicted clergymen from a church which held those in the grip of serfdom. Records were burned, and wealth was stolen. A chancellor from Cambridge University was similarly executed for fraud. Some rebels were able to take over Nottingham Castle, marching through the gates that were open to relive what happened at London's Tower of London. Other castles were seized in the same manner, as well as other aristocratic homes were demolished and others were executed. This happened all over England. Additionally, many of the targets be members of the Hospitallers.

It is evident it was a period of sort of communication and coordination between rebels. From the north of Yorkshire nearly on the same day there were peasant revolts. The repercussions of the rebellion was massive. In the entire nation, the king and the authorities took a stance on the smallest signs of discontent and disorder. The papers which were taken by a handful of rebels who had attended meetings with King were later thrown away. The promises were not kept and arrests were made and some were executed. Inquisitions were conducted. They were not just to snare the rebels but also to find the larger network of communications that was hidden behind the rebellion. There was an obvious belief that there was more to the revolt than the sudden and unpredictably flow of blood pouring over the heads of the peasants. Somebody, it was believed, was responsible for all this.

Chapter 7: The Shadow Organization Shadow

Organization

The aftereffects of Peasants' Revolution was brutal. While the majority of the information and debates of the time originate from people who had particular motivations to appeal to the king's favour There are ways we can examine the possible truth that lies beneath the propagandism and bias. For instance, the documents related to the inquiries and questions conducted by different aldermen and other government officials often includes the mention of a mysterious organisation. Although many rebels confessed that they were in fact angry at authorities, some were able to be referring to an unidentified group who sent messengers and representatives inciting discord and assisting in the rebels. The group was described in the official records by the name of the Great Society.

A book on the Freemasons is remiss without mentioning their Great Society. While we've gone over a lot already in this book but the benefits will soon come. The concept is to trace a path between the very first incarnations that were part of the Knights Templar, through to the Great Society which helped organize the Peasants rebellion, and on to the eventual emergence into the wider community of Freemasons and their eventual acceptance as element that is modern society. While some would suggest this could be a hint of a larger conspiracy theory, that a single organisation has been in charge of the political machinery in Western society for a long time but this isn't the case. The presence and significance that secret societies (of of which, the Freemasons are among the most famous in the present day) ought to be examined in a rigorous manner. To do this, understanding how the Freemasons of today might be linked to their medieval ancestors is crucial. To continue the research We should be asking ourselves: who was the founders of the Great Society?

When we examine the official accounts of the peasants' Revolution there are some aspects that are notable. The first is the role played by the King Richard II. Although he was still a teenager at his time Richard II has been portrayed in the media as being a leader, a powerful persona. He takes decisions, motivates people, and then eventually stifles the revolt. However, this is in the face of the facts. In reality, it was just at the age 23 that Richard actually ruled his kingdom. Prior to that, the kingdom was mostly governed by a regents' council, an elite group of men who made and took decisions for the king's behalf. In the unofficial account about Richard that have been handed down from generation to generation reveal the stammering, weak-willed teenager. Absolutely not the kind of person who rode into a rebellion and sounded confidently to them after slaying their leader.

The second reason is that the function that The role of Tower of London is somewhat uncertain. It was by far the most convenient area to defend in England to defend, particularly against a small group of rebels. What made it so easy to Wat Tyler to just walk through the town with a handful of soldiers? Why didn't he bother with establishing his own base after executing his men? Why would he bother even in the event that the meeting with the King had any possibility of solving the issues of rebels? It's more likely that the purpose of having a meeting with the King in Mile End was to remove the city's king instead of the rebels.

Then, the Tower to be attacked by Tyler the leader of the rebels who was not even able to take part in the discussion with King. Could be that the assault at the Tower was actually the real goal?

Another point to consider to consider, in the same vein: what was the reason that some of the most important members of the King's council left inside the Tower for rebels' execution? It is true that the Archbishop from Canterbury being kept in the Tower is plausible, given that the Archbishop had attempted to escape the Tower with a boat was launched in the morning. However, the reason Robert Hales was trapped behind in the Tower is a lot more difficult to understand. As the preeminent to the Knights Hospitallers, Hales was not only a seasoned battle commander, and one of the most skilled fighters in the kingdom however, he was the person who was expected to be selected to assist the king when faced with an enormous challenge to the Kingdom. Hales was a participant in the most recent Crusade with excellent successes. He was the leader of an order of monastic military knights. He was well-known all over the kingdom as an intimidating man and excellent soldier. Why would you leave such a man to be forgotten?

There are a myriad of questions. What was the reason the king did not return to the tower after the meeting with rebels? Did it happen by chance that his staff and household servants were in the tower in the first place? We are back to the belief that it was regents' council of the King instead of the king who made these the decisions. It is likely that they arranged these matters prior to the time and then simply took Richard around.

It's also useful to consider the role played by the king during his aftermath following the revolt. In many cases, royal pardons were granted. Cities that were host to rebels were granted amnesty, which allowed the residents to go back to their normal activities and for the incident to be forgotten. However, the amnesty was not available to all. There were 287 people specifically identified as not eligible for the amnesty. Other than those listed on the list who were already imprisoned following the military crackdown on rebels, the rest of them just vanished. They are not mentioned again in the records. Men like Henry de Newark and Richard de Melton were listed as part of the 287 list. 287 as well as being included in a royal writ which was released on December 10 1381. The men were sought for their role in the riots they taken part in riots in Beverly. The response of the local authorities was that the two men were not found in the region. They were gone.

So, the natural next step is to inquire about what they did. At a time when moving between cities and towns was far more complicated and less common and the loss of individuals who were not within the local sphere or influence area was more significant issue. It is interesting that the fact these people were only a handful of examples of the same with many of the people listed who were listed on the list of 287 seems odd in the context of. Certain historians draw a connection between the disappearance of the rioters as well as the disappearance of the Knights Templar seventy years beforehand. The two groups have a lot in common in that they were recently slammed by the authorities, sought out by both the government and the church as well and in dire in need of shelter as well as food and a place to find a place to hide. To have so many men quickly find shelter by using such dexterity is indicative of a planned escape plan or perhaps secure homes and bolt holes that are ready for those who would surely draw the ire of the government. The support, it has been claimed, was provided by the known as the Great Society.

However the response from the Church was instructive. In spite of the fact that the rebels removed the head of Archbishop Canterbury and replaced him, the church did not care about the direct punishment. In the end, it was the Church that began an anti-heresy campaign and the exact same sin which authorities claimed the Templars of having committed seven decades earlier. However, the real effect of the revolt on the church was not to be felt for quite a while but. The seeds for doubts and anger that arose in the Revolt which would then blossom fully during the Protestant Reformation.

However, as we've already mentioned the main mystery surrounding the Peasants' Rebellion is without doubt the shadow group that appeared to be in charge of arranging events and cooperating in the background. There was a certain degree of secret organization underlying the uprising is an assumption shared by the majority of historians, but they differ as to the precise extent and details of the mysterious group. Additionally, one of the major questions is whether the group was acting in directly in reaction to the political turmoil of 1381or in reality a pre-existing group that was beginning to act as a response to grievances and agendas that were held for centuries? Simply put did the organization exist as only a temporary response or a pre-existing group? Could the 287 people who were not granted amnesty from the amnesty were suspect to be members? Could this shadowy organization be the last remnants of Knights Templar, who had been hiding for seventy years?

The evidence is all in the fact that an organized, large-scale intervention against the authorities has to take a significant amount of planning. Due to the documents that were retrieved from bailiffs and sheriffs, we can confirm that authorities believed that the meetings were held secretly during the months prior to June. This could have taken a amount of work. Making a community of reliable individuals, screening members, and deciding on the agendas and locations for meetings is a challenge even when it is limited to a particular geographic location. Doing similar things across the medieval England would be extremely difficult.

The peasants Revolt was organized, smart, and well-organized, and motivated. A hidden society, one that could have created and sustain a system for clandestine communications across the nation without getting discovered, appears to have been beyond those of typical peasant. Even in small groups of three or two towns, the tools and resources available to the typical person working would likely be insufficient to be able to complete the task. Take into account the fact that the majority of people in the villages were not educated, and the extent of an organization starts to be apparent.

It is important to remember that, however hard an organization might be trying to keep it secret there were those who were trying to find the truth about them. Spies or traitors and double agents were out of the realm of possibility. In the course of responding the use of secret signals. These can be verbal gestures, pre-planned conversation signals, or even gestures. The most important thing is that in a community that is spread across England where agents and messengers do not communicate with one another this system must be standardized. This also shows an amount of resource and expertise that is far above the normal revolt.

But, in a day where it is simple to find a myriad of conspiracy theories, and frequently overextending theories of what a hidden society could be capable accomplishing, it is not forgotten that the Peasants Revolt wasn't solely planned in the hands of The Great Society. There were numerous motives, both political and social, behind the revolt. One of the most obvious was due to the Black Death and its aftereffects. The impact that the Plague affected the labor market was among the major factors behind the revolt and it is insincere to propose something similar to the notion that an organization deliberately introduced an epidemic in the country to set up conditions for a rebellion. They could not have been responsible for the corruption or attitudes of the church, or the laws and taxes made by the government of the King.

The person who was the coordinating force in the background of the Peasants' Rebellion is believed to have noticed the conditions and profitably capitalized on them while igniting the fires of revolt. By bringing old grievances and old issues in the community to voice and articulate these issues for everyone to listen to. They focused on anger and blame on their own ends. It is believed that Wat Tyler perished before that Revolt could achieve its objectives suggests that we'll never be able to determine what the mystery leader and the group truly desired. We are aware that the controlling hands of the rebels appeared to be dying alongside him, with the organizers slipping back to the shadows.

And where does this leave us? Although we believe there was a possibility that the Great Society was definitely authentic, we are still nearly seven centuries to separate us from the actual facts. In addition, the process of trying to discover evidence is not easy. Not only has only some of documents from the past even survived to the present time, but the ones which did survive are often composed from the viewpoint of the authorities. As we've seen, the society that was secret was adept at concealing itself from the authorities. We who are scouring for seven centuries later, are in a bind. Instead of evidence of that Great Society itself, we can see the mark of the institution. We see the footprints of the feet and not just the footprint itself. It is possible to interpret their existence by looking at the context as well as the surrounding environment and the government's response, more than any single item of proof. There isn't a smoking gun. There is no mention of one Great Society The sources are not willing to use the term "the one' as the sole source and instead refer to 'a' as the Great Society. We use only the name as"the" Great Society due to the fact that we don't have a other name.

In addition trying to prove the existence of such a society appears to be in contradiction terms. If it was truly secret and highly successful an organization that was secret would not be known to anyone other than its members. That's probably the reason there isn't any public record of secret society in the medieval period of England apart from that of Lollards (whose work is not directly related to this subject).

Now, at the very least, and slightly briefly, we get to our discussion of the Ancient Order of the Free and Accepted Masons. At the beginning it is imperative to state that there isn't any contemporary evidence that supports the existence for The Freemasons during the time of England during the time of the revolution. There is also no evidence in support of this, even though it is the responsibility to prove that is in the previous position. However, the evidence linking the Freemasons to the uprising stems only a few years after the fact.

In 1717 the shift took place in the manner that the Masons were run. In more detail in the future the Freemasons emerged from into the darkness and changed to a publicly-owned group. After this, it was that the Freemasons are a real group. However, that hasn't stopped writers on their experience as Freemasons to trace their history to a greater extent. A quick search on the internet or a glance through some of the less well-studied books on this subject will reveal people like Pythagoras, Julius Caesar, and other notable historical individuals as members of the Order or even Grandmasters. They are typically flights of fancies, and have no real basis connecting the speculation to actuality. These kinds of things aren't worth noting, other than acknowledging their speculation. Others, with slightly more moderate theories have been put forth by individuals such as King Solomon (the man who constructed the Temple Mount) the Temple Mount) and that his temple was the first one that was dedicated to Masonry. The more modern historians have labeled this as a similar exaggeration. But, that's not to suggest that the history of the Freemasons can't be traced to a number of centuries prior to the time they first came to the world's attention.

Many historians believe that the origins of the group today referred to by the name of Freemasons could be traced back to the middle ages. At the time there has been a suggestion that stone masons and other experts formed guilds (a known fact) and the guilds later changed into secret societies. This is among the most popular versions of the story of the founding for the Freemasons. It is enough to glance at the name to discover the obvious etymological connection between the masons' guild and Freemasons. How does this tie in with the peasants' Revolution as well as that of the Great Society that may have orchestrated the whole thing?

The historians have first pointed to the man who was alleged to be the leader of rebellion, Walter the Tyler (to provide the full title.) Like the many professions passed through the generations of fathers to sons in England in the past the surname given to the man (typically having the addition of the word 'the') would be an indication of the profession he was in. In a time when professions could be part of families for many years, and communities were comparatively small, these names were significant. Although their contemporary models have been severed from the professional aspects One only has to examine the surname of Wat Tyler to see that he could have been to have been a tradesman or at the very least the family of tylers who were trades-oriented (tilers).

Wat Tyler is an intriguing character of English history. It appears as if he is a blip, but Wat Tyler emerges to be the leader of one of England's biggest ever rebellions, involving thousands of peasants on a protest against the elite. He destroys a number of properties (including some that belong to the

Hospitallers) as well as burns numerous documents, and executes a number of individuals (including the archbishop of Canterbury and the Prior to the Knights Hospitallers). As soon as his arrival at the scene, he disappears. After a few days of being deemed one of the prominent individuals in the whole kingdom, he's executed and his head is shackled on a metal pole that is atop London Bridge. The total time in the spotlight was around eight days. Prior to that, we knew little about the man. Then, he turns into an icon.

There are rumors that Wat Tyler was using a fake name. Although his name could indicate a past in the field of roofing his obvious military skills and leadership abilities appear to render this irrelevant. It could be that he selected the name "Tyler" for motive, hoping to signal his status and importance to people who were aware of the significance of his name.

We will take a side trip into Masonic law. If you aren't familiar to the concept, it is a Masonic Lodge as an organization is a clear structure. Within each lodge are particular titles for certain roles and tasks. The title Tyler is one of these titles. In the framework of the context of a Masonic Lodge The person who holds the title Tyler is regarded as the enforcer and sentry or sergeant at-arms of the respective Lodge. He is responsible to scrutinize potential members and verify their credentials, ensure that the venue is safe, and after the meeting is taking place, he must be present outside the room , while holding an open sword. In contemporary terms it's essentially the position of a ceremonial one. In the old secret societies and in the past, when they existed in the shadows of (and often opposed against) the law and law, this was an important post. Tyler is the name of the post. Tyler for Masons is a reference to something extremely specific.

So, if we were to consider the possibility that there could be a connection (any whatsoever) to The Great Society and the group that would later become the Freemasons We can see how the term Wat The Tyler was much more than just a random pseudonym. For those who were aware the appearance of Wat Tyler as the leader of the rebellion could have been a sly sign of a sign of an appointed military leader, the one who could carry the sword and ensure discipline and success in the military. The relationship is hazy it is certainly speculation but nonetheless interesting.

Similar to the belief that Yorkshire was a major location for the revolt, specifically in York City. York in its own. York has been a major player in Masonry as well, with Masons in the 18th Century being convinced of the notion that York Lodge was the most important. York Lodge is the oldest in the United States. The origins of the Lodge is, according to the legend is dated back to the building of York Cathedral in medieval times. Through the 18th century it was it was the York Lodge would play a crucial part in the Freemasonry. Incredulous at the decision made by London Lodges to make publicly about the existence of their lodge in 1717 they spent the rest of the period distancing them from the southern counterparts and asserting their right to be in their own right, which is a crucial and privilege they believe was a right of members of the York Lodge for a long time "time has been immeasurable." To this, the unique role of York in relation to Freemasonry is reflected in the contemporary belief--especially in the eyes of American Masons, that York is the most authentic branch of Masonry. York part in Masonry has the highest quality, and most aligned with Masonic tradition.

It's not difficult to see that the Revolt was conceptually similar to many Masonic principles. If we consider the Revolt in a macro sense it is clear that it was a rejection of serfdom, the desire to be free and to release the chains of power-hungry relationships are very much in keeping with the many beliefs which are held in the hands of the Masons. Indeed, one of the central concepts of the order--known as the Landmarks of Freemasonry--requires that a Mason be a "free man born of a free mother." Serfdom, seemingly, would prohibit this. The fact that, by the time of the 15th century, nearly every male (at at a minimum the majority of White English male) in England could be thought of as "free" is employed by some to show that the mere existence of this requirement suggests that Masonry as an idea is extremely ancient. The fact that the Peasants Revolt might have been an act of protest in support of Masonic ideals but it's not evidence that any Great Society could be considered as a precursor or early form or a precursor to the Freemasons. However, it does provide some color to the notion that the Masons could exist (and were influential) way before the period which is generally accepted.

Perhaps the most compelling evidence linking our diverse strands in a single thread is shown by looking at a different kind of society in total. It is the key for understanding possible earliest signs of an Masonic secret society might be proven through the existence of Knights Hospitallers. The many attacks by rebels against Hospitaller properties as well as being executed by their previous (or leader) Sir Robert Hales is extremely instructive. Take, for example, George de Donesby. Although he was from Lincolnshire the man was taken into custody around 200 miles from home and admitted to being an associate of the Great Society. The reason for this is that the peasants in revolt in his town were particularly displeased with the conduct that their local leaders had displayed. They did not pay taxes, which could end up in a manor owned by the Knights Hospitallers. He is among the few people who could be directly linked with the history in the Great Society and also possessed an unmistakable resentment towards those who controlled the Knights Hospitallers.

Naturally, the series of rioters' assaults on Hospitaller properties shows that this was definitely an agenda-driven process. For instance, the move of the rioters, particularly those from north London to Highbury to try to burn down the Hospitallers manor that was newly constructed is an obvious sign that they were as a natural adversary of the rebels. The manor was located in the center of London with many possible locations, the rebels drove six miles to the north to take on Hospitaller properties. Similar instances can be seen throughout the nation in which rioters were granted a special allowances to target these homes. In Cambridge for instance there were rioters who rode for ten miles away from their route to set fire to the other Hospitaller manor.

It's been widely believed as a fact that the Peasants' Revolution was in part a protest against the corruption that the Church has. If this is the case, rebels definitely targeted religious and church buildings during their protests, especially when they were burning documents which could be employed by the government for spreading serfdom. However, the churches they targeted were owned and managed under the control of the Hospitallers. It was only the buildings that belonged to these Knights which the rebels intentionally searched for and then destroyed. There were other attacks that were usually isolated crime of opportunity. Rarely did rebels stray from their path apart from attempting to take over Hospitaller properties.

In fact, the only church that rebels didn't seem to have a desire to burn is the Hospitaller church located just across Fleet Street. Instead they took all the documents that could be found in the church and burned them on the street. It was a coincidence that the property been previously one of the Knights Templars' favored properties? Could there have been an intention to safeguard this church above all others, despite existence of Hospitallers? The church was dedicated at the time of 1185 Heraclius, who was then the patriarch of the city of Jerusalem under by the title of Knights Templar. The same patriarch also consecrated the Hospitallers properties in Clerkenwell and, possibly because that property was not belonging to the Templars, the rebels did not have a problem with burning the building down. Could it be an unintentional coincidence that the strikes by rebels were clear in their focus on one of the most enduring enemies from the Knights Templar? Could this be an act of revenge by an organization that had appeared to have disappeared and was then sucked completely out of the picture?

Even the smallest details such as the selection of uniforms among the rebels, suggest the possibility of a Templar influence. For instance, in places like Scarborough, Beverly, and York The rebels wore themselves in a white shawl covered in hoods and with the addition of a red accent. This kind of object suggest planning--it would have been difficult to design 500 of them immediately and then spread them over long distances, but it was strikingly similar to the clothes that the Templars themselves, wearing a white mantle that was adorned with an red cross.

A most fascinating sources is the demise of Jack Strawe. Strawe was among the top rebels as well as an aide for Wat Tyler. Strawe was arrested and brought to London in the course of which he was sentenced to be executed for his role in aiding in the organization of an uprising. Authorities tried to get an apology from him, however they were able to offer Strawe the opportunity of an Christian burial and the assurance that three years' worth of services would be offered in his honor. The only thing he needed to do was admit the "true reason" of the uprising. Strawe accepted and issued authorities the following statement. In his statement, he said that the goal was not just to gather an enormous crowd of ordinary people and take out any lords who would oppose them, but also to eliminate the Hospitallers. They were not just their property, but also their organisation. This hatred was not explained however there appears to be a single logical answer for those asking this question. Who could have disliked the Hospitallers to this degree?

It was a resentment that was simmering for a long time. Since the dissolution of Knights Templar in 1312, after 5 years of torture, and the investigations by various institutions, there was the issue of what should be done to the Templars vast business portfolio. A lot of people who were looking to disband the Templars sought the wealth to themselves, and they did however one of the biggest winners was Knights Hospitaller. It's clear the reason why a group that was snatched away and pushed into secrecy may be angry and dislike one of their main adversaries. Was this the motive behind the destruction of Hospitaller properties and being executed by the great prelate of the Order, Robert Hales? Could the Templars might have held an identical grudge towards the Catholic Church, the same institution that was founded, but then abandoned them, to the point that they disregarded their obligations to the Holy Sacrament, ignored ancient practices of the sanctuary or even executed an Archbishop from Canterbury? It's clear that the Templars could have been angry with each of these institutions and the Revolt offered them an possibility of obtaining some form of retribution.

It is possible that there could be as if there is a clear link towards that of the Templars from the writings that were taken of Bury St. Edmunds. One of the bloodiest locations of the Revolt that was exempted from amnesty. If you look into the archives of the period, Antonia Gransden's book highlights the fury that could have been sparked by Templars.

The chronicles adapt certain of the Templars the most famous and notable stories and depict the Benedictine writers changing their Knights into treasonous men , rather than heroic heroes. The narratives go as that they accuse the Templars for poisoning King Cyprus along with his family. It could be enough to cause a secret Templar force to rage and also hints at the propaganda campaign which was released in the aftermath of the Templars' loss. as the basis for some of the most extreme falsehoods regarding the Templars, Bury St. Edmunds may have experienced the violence that was brought on the town as a result of those of Benedictine monks.

The whole supposition of the suppositions brings us to a crucial issue. While the Peasants Revolt is often considered to be a failure, do we really believe this? If there truly was a Great Society -- which may be the descendents of the Knights Templar, providing advice, guidance and motivation did the Revolt actually a huge success for those who were behind the behind the scenes?

If we look at the viewpoint that of what is known as the Great Society and assume that they were connected to the Templars Then did demolishing Hospitaller Crown, Hospitaller, as well as Church property one of the primary objectives of the revolt? If yes the result could have been more than a small amount of success to be had. The destruction of huge amounts of precious properties, degrading records, and taking the wealth from famous opponents of the Templars will surely indicate that the Revolt might have been a successful one from a Templar perspective.

It's hard to accept. If we believe the notion of the Templars were in fact the Great Society or, at the very the very least, they were the foundational layer of it, then we have to think about how an organization that was either disbanded or forced underground for over sixty years could be so influential. Along with having several of their most influential commanders executed in the purge of the Templars and knights who were part of the order would have gotten older dramatically. Aged twenty for instance, could have reached the age of 90 at the time of the Revolt. They'd have to be lower-ranking members at the very minimum. It is unlikely that people like these could endure long enough to cause an uprising (especially when we consider other bizarre theories, such as the Templars holding their own Holy Grail and any attendant benefits that it could have).

Also, the notion that the Templars can continue to exist in secret for a variety of generations to come, but continuing to pursue their initial desire for revenge, is just as unlikely. Would a society like this be hidden in England for more than seventy yearsand be able to benefit from social and cultural changes that could eventually cause the Peasants' Rebellion?

Moving away from the details of the narrative for some time We can examine the facts:

* It is likely that there was some group (loosely organized) that were sympathetic to those who supported the Templars in England during the time of their demise. This can be seen in the greater number of individuals who could escape capture in England as opposed to other countries. The crown and the church later teamed up to locate the remaining Templars and found just three of them.

The Templars who were snatched in England in the initial round of arrests had the ability to escape prison. This implies that they had assistance, whether on the inside or on the outside.

* The first wave arrests in England occurred three months after the initial order was given across the continent. This gives those Templars in England the time to prepare as well as prepare their legacy as well as hiding places.

* In those three months during that time, the Templars might have created the new organization, which was a loosely organized group created to assist them in following the directives of the Pope.

Should such a group were to exist it would be established using the vast resources that the Templars could have and would need to fight even after the loss of the founding members. Therefore, it is well-funded and will likely change in the coming generations.

* If an organization would last for a long time it would be best to use simple objectives and goals would enable the organization to stay

focused even in the face of a lack of organization and the risk of being discovered.

However, where does this organization be found? Could it be possible that it is possible to discern a connection between the decline of the Templars and the revolt that erupted from the Great Society, and then the rise of Freemasons? We've already begun to consider what it is that could be possible for all three to have the same motives, and as we'll see later--how they are influenced by the same beliefs. In the near future they could be the Freemasons might even incorporate some of the Templars' terms and expressions into their very nature. However, in order to discover the truth behind this mystery, we'll have to examine the north of the frontier. The crucial element to the three groups, it appears to be located in Scotland.

Chapter 8: Scottish Roots

Scotland appears to be the common thread when it comes to discussing both the Freemasons as well as their Knights Templar. It is Scotland which is the site of both the demise of the Templars and the rise of the Masons but the exact nature of the change is a hazy, challenging part. Based on the person you think you are, the transition could have happened over the course of a couple of years, years, or even hundreds of years. In the next chapter we'll try to discover how the foundation was set through the Templars to establish the organization which would eventually be the Freemasons and how this might relate to the Great Society and the Peasants"Revolt. To achieve this, it is important to consider a moment to think about the current political climate in Scotland.

Relationships among Scotland and England isn't always smooth and, to put it mildly, a bit tense. In the past, both countries have been at war for a long time. A large portion of this was because of the actions of one man we have met in this novel, Edward I. Nicknamed the Hammer of the Scots, Edward spent a large portion of his time to solving the problems facing his northern neighbors. We've previously discussed Edward's role in restoring the country's status. We do not have the enough time to go into detail about the fascinating tale of his wars against Scotland. A brief summary is needed to set the stage.

Simply stated, Scotland wanted to be completely independent of English rule. There were clear reasons why England was not keen for this to occur. Relations between the Lords from Scotland as well as the English crown permitted an agreement that was a good fit for both ruling parties. However, the Scottish people were not happy. In the ranks one person stood up and took on the English. He was William Wallace. In modern cinema the majority of people have heard the story of Wallace and his ardent pursuit of freedom. Wallace was among his most effective Scottish battle commanders in the battle against English. In 1297, at the end, Wallace had led small Scottish army against massive English forces, and had triumphed.

However, Edward I was an imposing foe. He and Wallace engaged in battle and engaged in battle in the following years. The battles were fought against an overall geopolitical battle in the sense that Scotland attempted to gain the loyalty from France in addition to the Vatican and hoped that an alliance could ensure their independence. England stood up to England in the diplomatic arena also, when Edward made their own peace in 1303 with France at the time of 1303. Edward was an incredibly successful use of the force from the Templar Knights, finally won over Wallace when he persuaded his friends in the Scots to lie to Wallace. He was abandoned by a number of Scottish Lords William Wallace was caught and then executed in horrendous manner. Edward I appeared to have won , and earned him the nickname that was later engraved on his tombstone. He finally struck the Scots.

The monarchs who follow that would be of the greatest impact However. As powerful a leader Edward I was the people who followed him had no of his grit. When Edward II was crowned king of England the country, he was in an extremely delicate situation. In the northern part of England, Scotland had been engulfed by hate for the English. And to make matters even more difficult the rise of Robert the Bruce meant he had to face the possibility of becoming a Scottish King from his very own. Robert had killed his rival in the race for crown glory and was now launching the process of regaining Scottish independence. While he was initially a victim of defeat when Edward I was still alive, Robert abandoned his plans and was planning his revenge. His brutality against Edward I against the Scottish was to leave his successor an angry nation ruled by a formidable adversary.

In the South, the demise of Edward I had a variety of implications. In spite of the fact that Edward I was admired by the Prince Philip and the rest of France, Edward II was not a dazzling persona. In fact, it was Edward I's admiration as well as his use of the Templars that meant Philip could not take a stand against the group. Following the demise of Edward I and the death of Edward I, the Templars were no longer able to enjoy this security. Philip was aware of the vacuum of power that developed could now move. Alongside the Vatican Philip, he started the war in the direction of his fellow Knights Templar.

This leaves us with two institutions with resentments that are shared by both.

Scotland as well as the Knights Templar were both deceived by France as well as the Vatican. Following the fall from Edward I, the Templars were no longer a group of privilege in England. Inflicted with persecution by Philip's forces as well as the church and the church, they were forced to flee, escape the gaze of the world and seek out a place of refuge. Given their wealth and expertise, it appears like they could be accepted across the border in Scotland. Both bodies had similar enemies, and this made them allies.

Following the decrees of the Vatican to ban the Knights Templar, countries across Europe responded differently. Even though Templars in Paris were, for instance, were detained, tortured and killed, it wasn't the case for all members. The chiefs of the Templars were enticed to travel to France prior to the time that the order was given, and this resulted in that the leadership at the top (including the Grand Master) was executed, and at least 56 Templars burning alive only the one occasion in Paris. In France certain, the uprising against the Templars was brutal.

However, there was a greater threat in Spain and Portugal in particular there was a bigger danger. Muslim forces were attacking into the Iberian Peninsula from the south and the Templars military branch playing one of the key elements in fighting the invaders. In the end, local churches carried out their own inquisitions on the Templars. Although they had found that the French as well as the Italian clergy had obtained confessions during torture-that is, during which the Templars were said to have confessed to all sorts of things including urinating on the cross to profaning God's name--their Iberian counterparts concluded that their Templars in innocence. However, that didn't mean that they were able to continue their existence. Instead they were rebranded as locally-based Templars were rebranded, and then emerged as a supposedly new order called the Knights of Christ. One of the major differences in this new group was that they were accountable for the local King instead of the pope. They were the brand new Knights of Christ were permitted to continue fighting their fellow Muslim invaders.

In Germany however, things went differently. Hugo of Gumbach who was one of the leaders in the area for the Templars chose to don his battle gear and march with aplomb into the council held by the Archbishop from Metz. In the council, he made an official statement stating that Templars were free of guilt and that their great master was wrongly being accused. He even stated that, in fact that the culprit that it was Pope Clement V who was the evil group. Hugo said that he was no more dependent on the Holy See due to this. Like all the Knights Templar present they were uninvolved. So convinced was he was of his innocence that him along with the other knights wearing armor would be willing to go on trial by fighting those who believed in the opposite. The accusations dissipated quickly.

On Cyprus the pope's orders were even less important. Since Cyprus was the site is the site of Templar headquarters it took a long time for the prince who was in charge of Cyprus to accept the papal bull, and at the time the Templars were finally tried they were found innocent. The trial was so unpopular with Pope Francis that he promptly appointed his own group of inquisitors to Cyprus to conduct a second trial. However, there are there is no record of the outcome of the trial. In the meantime however the Templars were given plenty of time to prepare for Vatican's men.

In France the situation was not going the way Philip was hoping. One of the primary motives for his deposing the Templars - to steal their vast wealth to himself -- was proving to be difficult to fulfill. The riches he could had expected to find appeared to disappear. It was the Templar fleet, which was among the largest fleets in Europe was also out of La Rochelle. The 18 ships managed and owned by the Templars appear to have disappeared.

Any remaining wealth was to be officially transferred into the hands that of Hospitallers. In the end the The pope Clement V would declare that the wealth and assets of the Templars would be transferred into the new order excluding those who resided on the Iberian Peninsula, due to the threat of Muslim forces. This would be something that irked Prince Philip of the French monarch who hoped to see a different order will be established, with him as its leader, and which would be granted the riches that was the property of Templars. There could be an agreement with Philip however, since local monarchs would be given an opportunity to recover amount they paid for the torture, arrests, and deportation of Templars as well as figures that might appear to have come

171

from the air. The desire to please all by the church would be the basis for the campaign to begin the next Crusade in the near future.

Thus, even though their treatment towards the Templars differed across Europe but it was the circumstances that took place in Great Britain that pertains most to the story we're telling. In England the change in monarchy was noteworthy. The change from one the strongest monarchs in the country and one that was weak is a significant roles in the story.

There are numerous stories of The King Edward II, the king of England. One of the most well-known is the story of the young monarch's love life and the many historians who speculate that his real affection was not with the French princess who was his bride and a man by the name of Piers Gaveston. The couple's blossoming sexual romance been largely unnoticed by Edward I, as the king of old struggled hard against Scotland. The romance would later turn into an issue by father-son rivalry with anger so strong as to cause Edward I to strike his son and take him to the streets with his hair. Then, Gaveston was banished.

Naturally his successor King Edward II's first move was to release his love from the wrath of his exile. This set the stage for the new reign the king's council fighting for authority. Gaveston's part in this was to ridicule his advisors to his lover, causing some astonishment among the aristocracy in the country. The incident was distracting when papal orders were passed around. As Clement V requested that the court settle with the Templars however, the ruling class were distracted by the issue of how they would deal with Piers Gaveston. In this context, Robert the Bruce was returning to his independence war and the wedding that was scheduled for Edward as well as Isabella from France was the focus of many.

Pope Francis and Philip both pleaded with the English to speed up their investigation for the Templars. The new king was hesitant to believe in the allegations however. His father was an active advocate and an all-time ally to the Templars and their presence was a significant element of his childhood. He believed the accusations to be untrue and wrote to the other monarchs across Europe seeking their help regarding the issue. Before they could respond the formal papal decree came to him and Edward was faced with no other option.

However, he didn't was quick to act However. There was a time period of about a month between the time he received the decree and the persecution of those who were the English Templars. This was plenty of period for Templars to formulate plans. The king's men finally rode away from London to search for the Templars They found the knights had disappeared completely. A few stragglers were found. Additionally, the documents maintained by the order had gone along with them. The Templars treasure appeared to have vanished. The officers walked into the Templars London headquarters hoping to find a massive amount of money but they discovered just PS200 which was a tiny less than what was anticipated.

Then King Edward II was also gone. He had fled to France for the wedding of the Princess Isabella (twelve in age at that time) and given Gaveston as his successor. This meant that Gaveston -- to the astonishment of nobles, Gaveston was not just the ruler of the kingdom, but also responsible for prosecuting the Templars. Gaveston didn't seem to have any interest about his job, and attempts to detain any Templars during the time following the papal order were sloppy. Of the handful that were caught, a few were able to escape. It could be that there was an executed escape plan by the Templars or the individuals who conducted the search had no respect for the prosecutor. Most likely, it was the latter.

In England the Templars who were arrested were not subjected to torture. Even though they were imprisoned by when Edward returned to England and later they were not being subjected to the same adversities as those who were captive Templars in the continent. This angered the pope to the point that the pope sent his own torturers to England to perform the job and threatened excommunication to anyone who assisted those Templars by any means. Although Edward put some limitations on the torturers who worked in England, such as no mutilations, for instance--he nonetheless bowed to the supreme authority of the pope. Even though this appeared to get no confession from the handful of Templars who were in jail, the practice did have an effect of distancing those who were hidden away from the authorities' eye.

While England eventually gave in to the pope's wishes, Scotland was a different story. The pope attempted and failed to get Templars in Scotland detained. Even though it was true there was evidence that Robert the Bruce did make some minor arrests in the beginning in 1308, the constant battles with the military meant that if he was confronted by a well-trained and efficient soldier, such as an armored knight, he was more likely to be recruited rather than to punishment. Robert was uninterested in any possible Crusade and didn't even care about monastic military organisations, and cared less about Philip the Philip of France and the Pope and was aware of the dangers developing in the south in the midst of Edward II prepared to resume his father's fight to end Scottish independence. In this regard it was reported that he had cast off the papal decree regarding the Templars. It was not announced in Scotland. It was a sign to be that Scotland was a legal refuge for fledgling Templars.

This meant that in the event that a Templar knight be in a legal dilemma in England or Europe in the future, he would not only hope to find refuge in Scotland and could received with open arms provided he agreed to be a part of Robert Bruce's military. Since the Scottish cavalry of the time was thought to be a small number and in quality, well-trained and equipped knights were crucial.

In 1313 England stood in in a precarious situation. A long-running dispute between Piers Gaveston as well as the Nobles resulted in the lover of the king being executed. As the nobles tried to reassert influence over Edward II, the king's father-in-law--Philip of France--advised that he should ratify his allegiance to the church. This was the time to embark on the newly announced Vatican Crusade. The previous year the same council had officially disbanded Templars in one and only way declared a plan to take back this Holy Land in the name of Christendom. Despite England promising to assist but to help, doing so would have been suicide. In the event that the country's finest combatants as Robert the Bruce stood in the face of Scotland could have ruined the advancement Edward I was so determined to make. In the midst of the Crusade was being announced, Robert was moving through Scotland and taking over castle upon castle. If Edward was looking to restore his position in the kingdom - and should he choose to launch an effective military campaign for that, the Crusades were not the ideal opportunity that he required. Instead, he'd have to take on the Scottish.

So Edward formed a force of 25,000 soldiers to go north to conquer Scotland completely. In his army the King of England had 5,000 cavalry as well as 10,000 archers. To counter, Robert the Bruce was capable of assembling 10,000 soldiers. However, Robert was aware that the English were on the way. Before Edward and his army began arriving the Scottish were able to choose the battlefield. While the English marching for miles and miles getting tired and hungry The Scottish took up their positions and ensured that they had enough food and well hydrated. It was the case that Robert set his army in the line between the moving English in the southern part of Scotland and the only remaining English outposts within the region, Stirling Castle. This means that Edward was unable to replenish his supply before meeting with the Scottish army.

When it was time to plan for the fight, Robert was influenced by everything that he gained through William Wallace. He dug up potholes in the field in order to deter English knights armed with weapons and then hid the men who carried twelve-foot spears to fend off the horses who might be chasing the Scots. They were hidden in a secluded area, concealing their presence. Wallace was deceived when his cavalry headed by one of the unhappy nobles and had left him in a crucial moment. Doing his best to avoid this fate again, Robert put himself in the top of Scotland's small group of knights in armor. According to legend, the majority of the cavalry was comprised of fledgling Templars who had fled north and swearing loyalty to Robert. The fight would enable them to get a bit of revenge on the one who betrayed them to the pope.

It was a well-known Scottish victory. When the English army was beaten back by the Scottish army, they turned around and fled. The decisive moment came when the supporters of the Scottish camp--the men, women and others who were not combatants had taken to arms and infiltrate the English who had assumed that this was a new surge from Scottish reinforcements. The fugitive army was defeated by the English, with England losing nearly 15,000 troops, as compared the Scottish losses of only 4,400.

This Scottish triumph was loud that it brought the end of English control over Scotland for almost 400 years.

Additionally, the massive magnitude that was the English defeat had left Edward II's realm in chaos. The nobles who were enraged by the poor leadership of their king and incompetence, began to assume more authority to themselves. In the United States the deterioration of order and law signified that outlaws started to roam the streets. This was the time of the adored outlaw heroes, including men like Robin Hood who fought against the corrupt rulers and took advantage of the rich. In the end, the consequences of the defeat were so devastating and devastating for Edward II. He would be deprived of his throne. He would not only not be king anymore, yet he was sabotaged by his wife as well as his nobles, the latter summoning an army of mercenary soldiers and the latter embracing said army with a warm welcome. In 1327, on the 22nd of September Edward had been executed. It was so funny for the executioners in dealing with the homosexual king , that they chose to make one last insult. The method used to execute the king was the smacking of a red hot iron to and spitting directly into Edward's rectum. The throne was then handed over to Edward III -- at the time still a young man - would be the next king to take the throne. It was Edward III's reign of success that was the catalyst for the Peasants' Revolution.

Where does this leave what happens to the Templars as well as the Freemasons? According to legend, they'd be located in Scotland. It was so disastrous during the reign that of Edward II that he did not just lost Scotland for decades however, his actions were instrumental in deporting off the federally banned Templars north. When they first arrived they'd have had to remain hidden. In the end, their mere existence was considered to be an insult to God. But their wealth, capabilities in the military and even their presence proved to be a blessing for the Scottish King. Therefore, in order to hide the secret Templars had to alter their organisation. They weren't an order of knights from the military in the traditional sense they were now an unofficial secret society. They had a plan to retaliate with vengeance, which needed to be slapped. Although they were still in hiding, their mindset should change from those who were on the run to those in hiding, from dominant men of power to cold and calculated powerful players. While they hid into the shadows they would have Templars had to establish a formidable secret society. They were still pursuing their ambitions would they have been an organization that would have become the Great Society which would trouble England seventy years after?

Conclusion

In the beginning in the Christian faith, believers were required to keep their faith as a secret. They were forbidden from practicing their faith and amidst the finest examples of a society that was secret. To connect with each other they adopted logos. The fish image--a basic shape, which is popular today-- became a card that was used to call friends and fellow Christians. It also gave them an explanation of the story, which allowed any person with a fish picture to say they were fishermen rather than an adherent to an unregulated religion. However, even after Christianity was accepted as a religion but this image was still. The meaning of the fish changed, in essence because it became the card used to identify an underground society. Fish was once an excuse for cover stories as a way to stay alive while being pursued by authorities. There are many different ways that it's similar to the notion to The Templars or the Freemasons.

As we've learned within this volume, there's numerous circumstantial evidence to suggest that the demise of the Knights Templar coincided with the creation of an underground group that was based in Great Britain. The wanted Templars may have linked themselves with a tiny Scottish mason's guild and masons, utilizing their symbols and symbols to cover a story to escape the scrutiny of authorities. Similar to how a guild would secure trade secrets, Freemasons were created to safeguard the lives of Templars in hiding. The principles they defended and carried into the making of the Freemason philosophy that would endure to this day. Although Freemasonry today isn't hidden in the same way as Christianity was able to become mainstream but the legacy of Templar influences is still evident similar to the symbolism of the fish can be seen in nearly every church across the globe. Although the current structure is quite different, it doesn't make a difference to look back at the past.